GARDEN PARTY

GARDEN PARTY

COLLECTED WRITINGS 1979–1999

ROY STRONG

Drawings by Julia Trevelyan Oman

FRANCES LINCOLN

Frances Lincoln Limited
4 Torriano Mews
Torriano Avenue
London NW5 2RZ

British Library cataloguing-in-publication data
A catalogue record for this book is available from the British Library

ISBN 0 7112 1458 1

Set in Garamond and Trajan by
Frances Lincoln Limited
Printed in Hong Kong

1 3 5 7 9 8 6 4 2

In Memoriam

GEORGE CLIVE
Friend & Gardener

CONTENTS

PREFACE

In 1979, the year of the great exhibition of the history of British gardening at the Victoria & Albert Museum, the late Graham Rose, gardening correspondent of *The Sunday Times*, asked me to write what I thought of the Chelsea Flower Show. Over the years since I have continued to write occasional pieces for newspapers and magazines, as well as being for a period the *Sunday Telegraph*'s gardening columnist. Even when writing what was essentially journalism, I always conceived of each piece as an essay, as literature, conscious that I was attempting to contribute to a great tradition of garden writing which is almost unique to this island. Each time I set out to write something which stood up beyond the transient moment. To me the richness of our garden writing inheritance has always resided in the fact that it embraced a wider cultural perspective, making the reader aware of the links that the art of gardening has with the other arts and with history. I was conscious when selecting and arranging the pieces here, several of which are new, that they embodied just such a coherent philosophy and they are presented in the hope that such a vision might be more fully shared and sustained.

Once again I wish to express my gratitude to my indefatigable editor, Julia MacRae, and my delight that I share these pages with my wife, Julia Trevelyan Oman. I owe the title of this book to Beatrix Miller.

Roy Strong
The Laskett, 2000

WHAT IS A GARDEN?

Most of us never ask ourselves a very basic question: what constitutes a garden? As far as we're concerned, it is just something that is attached to where we happen to live, an area of land, in the main small and getting smaller, jutting out before and aft of a dwelling house. The terrain is generally flat and enclosed by a fence or, if we are lucky, a wall or clipped hedge. We fill that enclosed space or alter what exists there already with items from a visual vocabulary derived from looking at other people's gardens or from what we have seen in books. Maybe we are in love with cottage gardens, in which case it is roses round the porch and burgeoning, muddled, relaxed borders brim full of old-fashioned flowers. Or, perhaps, we might be entranced by formality and orchestrate the space with built structure and clipped evergreens arranged in carolling symmetry. In this way, most people's garden-making is bound by convention and fashion fed by the explosion of garden design books. The options are in fact quite narrow. In the two design books I wrote, which were aimed at offering the average gardener the available options for the small garden, I was hard put to it to assemble as many as twenty contrasting formats.

That in itself should make us pause, for it means that today we think about a garden purely in terms of design and style. I was sharply reminded of that fact by a passage which occurs in a book by a great Italian Renaissance scholar, Eugenio Battisti, when he describes what the garden encompassed for that age:

As part of its ability to play with the human senses, the Renaissance garden is an intriguing conceptual system ... The garden is a place of pleasure, the *locus amoenus*, filled with joy, but it resounds in love laments of poets; it is a place of feasts, entertainment of friends ... of sexual and intellectual freedom, a setting for philosophical discussions, and a restorative for both the body and the soul. It is a measured and well-ordered model of the universe, an experiment in immortality, a never-ending apparition of spring. It assumes the function of a sculpture gallery, a *pinacoteca*, a horticultural encyclopedia *in vivo*, a centre of botanic and medical research, a theatre for imitation, competing with nature on nature's terms and conditions. Finally, it is a perpetual source of moral instruction.

It is mentally challenging to take in even one aspect of the complexities which governed and motivated the creation of the great gardens of the Renaissance and of the centuries that followed. What this passage highlights, however, is that style and design were once profound expressions of ideas and meaning and not just fashion options like buying this season's clothes. Some of what Battisti lists we recognise as being still with us, like the garden as an horticultural encyclopedia or as a setting for sculpture. Others defeat us, like a garden giving moral instruction or providing an arena for intellectual debate.

What to my mind it drives home is that in the late twentieth century we have reduced the making of a garden almost wholly to a design option. We have impoverished garden-making by taking away meaning. And where gardens do have meaning – as, for example, do those created by Ian Hamilton Finlay or Ivan Hicks – we are unnerved and we turn away, feeling them to be uncomfortable aberrations, whereas they speak from the heart of a great tradition as it has descended through the centuries but in terms of their own age.

As we enter a new century we should ask ourselves, haven't we lost something along the way? In the quest for an answer I turned to Charles W. Moore, William J. Mitchell and William Turnbull Jr's *The Poetics of Gardens* (1989), a book which was eulogised for reminding us 'that the most rewarding experience of the garden and the park is to see them as works of art', as against the current fashion of viewing them as 'providing space for recreation, for urban decongestion, therapeutic contacts with nature, the presentation of ecosystems'. So here we have, usefully listed, garden roles as seen at the close of the twentieth century, ones reflective of a democratic age where social use comes high but embracing also the rising concern for the environment. All these have triggered and conditioned the types of garden, both public and private, which we have seen created now.

In their view, 'Gardens are rhetorical landscapes ... they are composed to instruct and move and delight (Cicero's definition of the rhetorician's duties). We can read gardens for content, and we can analyse the devices of structure and figure and trope by means of which they achieve their effects.' Gardens are then considered as falling into one of four categories: those 'where the relationship of things is so moving or so clear that the rest of the world is illuminated for us'; those which act as vehicles of collections, from plants to sculpture; those which call for the visitor to be a voyager; and, finally, the ones which use pattern to 'express some vision of order' akin to verse.

I am not sure that this gets us much further, for although the plea is to see a garden as primarily a work of art, that again is formulated essentially in design terms. I don't see much sign of the rhetorician's duty to instruct, which brings me back to meaning. On that topic, a weird collection of articles published in 1990 on *The Meaning of Gardens* (edited by Mark Francis and Randolph T. Hester Jr) left me even more confused. This collection of papers from a conference staged at the University of California in 1987 only confirmed me in my belief that all the maddest people just kept going west until they came to the Pacific and were forced to stay put. We are whirred through the garden as idea, place and action, and then confronted with the five impulses which they view as defining today's garden-making: faith, power, ordering, cultural expression and healing.

Although a monument to academe-speak, the papers at least move from a premise of meaning, however dotty some of it is. What they did reinforce in my mind was how little most garden books ever touch on that subject – one which, through the rise of garden history, we are made more and more conscious of as the riches of allusion, which the garden as a vehicle in times past had, become ever more clear to us. That in turn makes me more and more conscious that as we progress into the new millennium the old clichés into which we have become stuck are being challenged from the evidence of the firmer ground of the past. The enormous success of anything to do with Derek Jarman's strange personal paradise, created on a desolate expanse of shingle facing the nuclear power station in Dungeness, Kent, signals that many are ready for startling changes as to what constitutes a garden, allowing for far more fantasy and individuality of expression than we have been accustomed to.

So I now come full circle, back to where I started with the question 'What constitutes a garden?' *The Shorter Oxford English Dictionary* defines a garden as ' … an enclosed piece of ground devoted to the cultivation of flowers, fruit or vegetables'. In terms of what we now know about Japanese rock and gravel gardens alone that definition no longer works. What constitutes a garden in the coming years will, I think, increasingly reflect the direction of our libertarian society, which focuses on safeguarding minority views. If someone states that his personal notion of a garden is a series of found objects from old tin cans to discarded animal bones scattered across an expanse of concrete it will be no longer challenged but accommodated. It will be his right to define that as his garden. What constitutes a garden, therefore, will reside henceforth in the mind of the person who creates it. It may defy every convention and style pumped out by the glossy garden books and magazines but it will be a personal paradise for its owner. Neither more nor less. The result will be experimental chaos but oh, how exhilarating!

GARDENS OLD

M y response to gardens came late – I was past thirty-five, I'm afraid. I can only partly explain that by the fact that I was brought up in a 1920s terrace house in north London and the garden 'belonged' to my father. It was touched by any other member of the family only at their peril. Alas, he became early on a symbol of everything I wanted to reject, gardening included. That, however, never impeded a passion for old houses and so my eyes were firmly turned inwards, fixed on to pictures and tapestries, panelling and plasterwork, furniture, china and silver. Occasionally I must have peered out of the windows but my eyes were firmly shut.

When they opened, after marriage, it was with all the force of an evangelical conversion, one which had begun to stir earlier when Cecil Beaton would walk me around his garden at Reddish House in Wiltshire. Suddenly I went into complete reverse, preferring to comb every nook and cranny of a garden rather than explore the shadowed interior of a house. From the outset it was never the landscape era but earlier periods which excited my imagination. I stood enraptured at the vast clipped yews at Packwood House, Warwickshire, which depicted the Sermon on the Mount; or wondered at the trim canals and espaliered fruit trees at Westbury Court, Gloucestershire; gazed in admiration at the great borders along the terraces of Powys Castle, in Montgomeryshire, with their lead shepherds and shepherdesses gesturing towards the hills of Wales. Knot and parterre, statue and gateway, maze and pleached avenue cast their spell, one intensified by a passion for Italy. So the discovery of the great Italian gardens fired me in all their crumbling glory, and from them my interest fanned outwards to embrace the baroque gardens of northern Europe.

Gardens are the harvest of peace and security. The lure of old gardens resides in that fact, aligned to timelessness. The centuries come and go, nations rise and fall, war alternates with peace, nature takes over and then is brought to heel, but still those gardens somehow go on exerting their magic.

THE PALACE OF HET LOO

I first visited Het Loo, in the Netherlands, in the spring of 1979. It was then a building site, the palace was under scaffolding, the land around devastated by the excavation needed to skim off the tons of earth that in the early nineteenth century had obliterated one of the great gardens of the baroque age, that laid out for William III and his English wife, Mary. This was my earliest contact with garden archaeology on a stupendous scale. As we trudged through the mud, a Dutch colleague would bend down and pick up, for instance, a piece of coloured gravel. What we were looking at was a precious sample that enabled those restoring the garden to select the correct colour for the gravel of one of the great parterres. At intervals, whole sections of the old layout would be revealed beneath the overlay: marble fountain basins, fragmentary flights of steps to terraces, a stone edging for a rivulet.

In this way I was present at the initial stages of what must be the greatest garden re-creation project undertaken this century. I am still overcome by the act of faith and the generosity of the Dutch government in funding this extraordinary venture, which eventually opened to the public in June 1984. The result is a garden experience unparalleled in Europe, for here you can walk through a baroque garden in its youth. The other great baroque gardens that have survived inevitably look tired and weather-beaten, while at Het Loo all is new, from the glistening highlights on the fountains to the fruit trees that are still being trained. There is all the exhilaration of walking into the past, combined with the immediacy of the fact that what we see is very much of the present. I go there, not just for a nostalgic trip, but for the joy it gives me as a gardener and for what I can learn on each visit that is relevant to garden-making today.

Let me set the scene. William bought Het Loo in 1685 in order to build a hunting lodge, but it quickly developed into something much grander under the aegis of the Dutch architect, Jacob Roman, and the Huguenot designer, Daniel Marot. Het Loo belongs to an age which still worked from Renaissance ideals that linked house and garden by means of a central axis and by the symmetrical arrangement of the rooms indoors and the parterres and fountains outdoors. Governed by the science of geometry, the result is one of harmony. Much learned ink has been spilled on what constitutes the Dutch style within the baroque idiom, but put that to one side in your enjoyment of the garden. What it does have, which its French counterpart lacks, is a kind of intimacy amid the assertive splendour.

More than any other garden, Het Loo reminds me of the importance of pattern at ground level, doubly necessary on a flat site where the changes of level can at best be minimal and contrived. Climb to the roof of the palace and look down on the stunning spectacle of clipped grass and box, with coloured gravels orchestrated into ordered and yet swirling baroque patterns whose punctuation marks are statues. Do not be surprised if the patterns look vaguely familiar, because you will have seen them indoors in the marquetry, the textile designs and the wrought-iron work – a reminder of a tradition which garden designers have mostly forgotten in this century, that gardening and the decorative arts shared a common repertory of ornament and pattern. How little we have done about this, and yet exponents of abstract art and post-modernism have given us an abundance of garden ideas, if only we had the imagination to put them into practice. Notice how the patterns in the parterres can be seen not only from the windows, but also from the raised terraces that surround three sides of the main garden.

These terraces have another lesson for us about that British garden monomania, grass. That ingredient, thought to be the key element in the English landscape style, enjoyed an even more exalted status in these formal gardens. On the gravelled terraces there are long, flat rectangles of grass. Within their period they epitomised one of the ultimate sensuous garden experiences – treading greensward underfoot. In the age before the lawn mower, close-clipped grass demanded a high maintenance commitment and was the height of luxury. Look down and observe how it was used in a way we would never think of today, cut into patterns with gravel as a foil, *gazon coupé*, as it was known. Parterres are a wonderful and neglected garden element, unashamedly artificial, ordering nature into patterns that change with the seasons and the light. From the moment one is planted, the pattern is there to enjoy. And they do not have to be historical pastiche. Het Loo was not, in its time; it was boldly planting the latest fashions in pattern.

The treillage, instead of being painted white or green, is an unusual and satisfying green-blue colour, which urges a reconsideration of our clichéd use of colour for built artefacts in gardens. Earlier ages were much bolder. There are plant supports in the same colour; I was told that it was almost certain that each would originally have been topped with a golden ball or crown.

But what about flowers? Het Loo is a healthy reminder of how spoilt we are, with cascades of bloom trailing in abundance. I do not think that I would want to copy a seventeenth-century planting, but I am glad to experience the degree of concentration which our forebears brought to plants. Every one is about three feet from its neighbour, and was meant to be contemplated as much for its horticultural attributes as its aesthetic ones. And then there were the exotics, such as lemon trees in vast containers, which wintered indoors and were brought outside for the summer and arranged in patterns around the parterres. For anyone interested in historic plants, this is a living encyclopedia of what was grown at the time. Usefully, each is meticulously labelled.

Although there are two stupendous plantings, for spring and for summer, it is worth going at any time of the year. The lessons to be learnt about structure and pattern make it a garden for all seasons.

HAMPTON COURT: THE PRIVY GARDEN

In 1987 a fire ravaged the King's Apartments of Hampton Court Palace, a catastrophe which in fact was to turn into a blessing, for it triggered a massive restoration programme of the historic interior, the first phase of which opened in 1992. A year before that the decision had been made to take the restoration out to embrace the gardens around. The rooms within had been restored to how William III would have known them when they had just been finished, the crowning touch to Sir Christopher Wren's new palace. Meticulous research ensured accurate redecoration in terms of paint effects, curtains and upholstery, and the Royal Collection returned the original furniture. The result was a triumph. Could that be repeated when extended to what should be seen from the windows? The King's Privy Garden is one of the great garden sites of the United Kingdom, with a history going back to the first Tudor garden planted for Henry VIII in the 1530s. What was going to be put back was a vast formal parterre of a kind which did not survive the onslaught of the landscape style. How would both media and public respond to such a revolutionary putting back of the hand of the clock?

In the event, and contrary to expectation, the opening of the restored baroque Privy Garden at Hampton was remarkable as much as anything for the unanimous acclaim with which it was received. That would not have been so twenty years ago. The restoration, besides being a triumph for painstaking research, archaeological, archival and botanical, marked also a significant turning point in the British perception and appreciation of the formal garden.

As recently as the middle of the 1980s, when the lime walks in the large Fountain Garden were replanted, there had been a battle royal over the felling of what were viewed as sacrosanct ancient trees. Even in the case of the Privy Garden, to avoid another of these public rows erupting, as many as possible of the old plants were carefully moved and saved, among them fifty-foot-high hollies which had begun their lives as neat clipped cones in William III's garden.

When, in 1992, I was filming a television series on the history of the royal gardens, I did a sequence stopping ordinary visitors to the palace and asking them whether they would like to see the baroque garden reinstated. The idea was greeted by everyone without exception with utter horror. To put back the baroque garden, wiping out old loved spreading trees, spacious lawns and lush herbaceous borders in favour of something seen as stiff and foreign, alien to the traditions of the country, was viewed as an unfriendly un-British act. So what has happened to reverse this attitude?

For that we have to reconnoitre back in time to the post-war era. The formal garden was then totally out of fashion, for it was the time when the tenets of Dame Sylvia Crowe pertained. She argued that the basics of all good garden design, even for a small suburban back yard, were those of 'Capability' Brown. This was the age of the serpentine line and the island bed. It was a period, too, which viewed formality of any kind as not only labour intensive but also unwelcoming in what was the increasingly relaxed era of the post-war socialist welfare state. Formality was tarred with the brush of a fast-vanishing age of hierarchy and deference.

It was only very gradually that the ground was to begin visibly to shift. The National Trust began to restore and re-create period gardens. In 1955 a box and gravel parterre based on contemporary sources was laid out in front of the seventeenth-century hunting lodge Ashdown House, Berkshire. In 1963 followed the garden of Mosely Old Hall, Staffordshire, this time a copy of a knot of 1640 surrounded by other features taken from old gardening books. These represented some of the earliest moves suggesting that a period house should also have a period garden. At the same time there were those who were advocates of formality in contemporary garden design. The greatest exemplar was the decorator John Fowler in his garden at King John's Hunting Lodge at Odiham, in Hampshire, with its pleached limes and strict geometry.

Then came the contribution of garden history to the change in climate. In 1966 the Garden History Society was formed, but that discipline was not to gain real momentum until after 1979, when the Victoria & Albert Museum staged the first major exhibition ever devoted to the history of British gardening. This was a watershed, for after that date the subject took off. Not only were historic gardens listed for the first time but more garden restorations got under way; and by the close of the 1980s enthusiasm for preservation of the country's garden heritage resulted in the county Garden Trusts being established.

More than that, taste began to change. The country house look in interior decoration dominated the 1980s and with it burgeoned an interest in their gardens. Those in the vanguard of forming popular garden style began to respond and pioneer a return to formality and the use of good built and evergreen structure. Books began to appear which advocated the style. The first was a curiously unnoticed one by David

Hicks on *Garden Design* (1982), which was a hymn to formality; it was to be Rosemary Verey's *Classic Garden Design* (1984) which captured the public imagination. My own *Creating Small Formal Gardens* (1989) was the first book wholly on the topic to be published since Blomfield's *The Formal Garden in England,* which appeared in 1892. Visitors to the Chelsea Flower Show saw sculpture and topiary multiply, as there was also an increasing realisation that formality was not, with the advent of modern machinery, that labour intensive.

My own bookshelves tell the story. In 1973–4, when we began laying out what garden designer Rosemary Verey has described as the largest formal garden made in England since 1945, I could find no books in print to tell me how to do topiary. The only book I eventually obtained was Nathaniel Lloyd's *Garden Craftsmanship in Yew and Box*, published in 1925. Then, at the close of the 1980s, they came in a flood: Geraldine Lacey's *Creating Topiary* (1987), A.M. Clevely's *Topiary* (1988) and David Carr's *Topiary and Plant Sculpture* (1989).

This is the broader context into which the restoration of the Privy Garden at Hampton Court should be fitted. It had, of course, a precursor in Het Loo, but that made little impact on the British public – most of them had not seen it and many of those who had disliked it intensely. When I took a group there in 1992 I was told that its predecessor had walked out of the garden in utter horror. To avert a repetition of this I talked at length to the group telling them how to look at such a garden. It worked and they loved it.

All of this signals that the moment was right to undertake the Hampton Court restoration, although Dr Simon Thurley and his colleagues shrewdly embarked on a long series of public consultations to persuade both public and press that they were doing the right thing. The fact that I wrote the first article to advocate the garden's restoration in *The Financial Times* as long ago as 1978 is some indication of the long haul it took to achieve it. By 1996, however, when the restored garden was opened to the public, everything was in place to ensure its success: garden history and archaeology had come of age, coinciding with the public's increasing interest in and appreciation of the earlier formal styles.

That success was aided by something which came as a complete surprise: that the final result was so different from Het Loo. William III's parterre at Hampton Court turned out to be an accurate reflection of the long English obsession with grass, for it consisted largely of patterned flat areas of perfectly cut turf adorned with statues. The Privy Garden parterre in fact falls squarely into John James's definition of 'A Parterre After the English Manner' in his *The Theory and Practice of Gardening* (1713). What separates it from the more pedantic 'plats' which appear all over the place is the cut-work and the encompassing flower borders. These make the final effect very different from the *parterres de broderie* at Het Loo which are far harder in feeling and appearance. The flower borders also look different: the Dutch are rather sparse in effect with quite large spaces between the plants, the English far more profuse and floriferous, which tempers the rigid formality. One must add to that the caveat that the planting is still in the experimental stage and subsequent research could modify the effect.

Once the garden was unveiled there was a keen recognition of the huge architectural gain. For the first time for two hundred years, Wren's masterly façade could be seen not only from the garden but also from the river bank. The glorious Tijou ironwork screens came into their own, providing a lacy *clair voyée* in both directions. There was above all an overwhelming realisation that the correct scale had been reinstated. The palace façade once more presided over a garden instead of having a jungle towering over it.

In addition there was a bonus for the interior of the palace, for inside and out had been conceived as one by the king's master-designer, Daniel Marot. To look down on the pattern from the Privy Chamber was to realise the complex interplay between the two, encompassing not only the shapes utilised but even the flowers, which could be growing in the *plates-bandes* as well as painted on one of the ceilings.

The restoration of the Hampton Court Privy Garden can be seen in one aspect as a reflection of the renaissance undergone by the formal garden in Britain over the last twenty years. In that perspective it is an affirmation and an acceptance of a *fait accompli*. It is not a harbinger of what is to come in new garden-making. That, I think, presages quite other directions responding to impulses as varied as the need to preserve wildlife habitats and species as well as native plants, and the shock waves of Derek Jarman which strike at the heart of Jekyllesque neo-romanticism. But that in no way diminishes the achievement at Hampton Court. In England it epitomises garden restoration's coming of age and the public's ability to accept varieties of historical garden style in the same way that they now take for granted successive styles of architecture and interior decoration. In that sense there has been nothing but gain out of the exercise by absolutely everyone concerned.

THE CHELSEA PHYSIC GARDEN

I am sitting in an arbour of sweet bay with cascades of purple flowers of thyme sprawling on either side of me. Neat brick and gravel paths stretch in a grid ahead, punctuated with domes of clipped box at the intersections. I am in a herb garden.

Near by the orris is in bud and the feathery leaves of tansy are pushing up fast as my eye falls on a notice which warns me not to touch the plants in one bed for they are poisonous ones, used for medicinal purposes – foxgloves, deadly nightshade, monkshood and lily-of-the-valley.

In a way this tableau is at the heart of a largely forgotten magical enclosure, the Chelsea Physic Garden. There is nowhere else that I know of in central London where it is possible to stroll in a seventeenth-century garden once visited by the gardener and writer John Evelyn, who recorded it in his diary. Chelsea was then famous for its gardens. Not far away were those of Sir Thomas More and Sir John Danvers, the man John Aubrey (of *Brief Lives* fame) describes as brushing his beaver hat on the thyme and hyssop in order to perfume it.

Both those gardens have long since vanished, but the Chelsea Physic Garden, founded in 1673, is still with us, a precious fragment of this country's garden history.

The reassessment of our garden heritage through the growth of garden history as a serious discipline has been one of the most exciting developments of recent years. That reawakening combined with the necessity to secure its future financially led to the rediscovery of the Chelsea Physic Garden.

Walled gardens always remain mysterious, but they can equally remain forgotten. Out of sight is out of mind, and the decision taken in 1983 to open the garden to the public is therefore greatly to be applauded, as also is the one to make its premises available for activities as varied as the sale of antique garden ornaments and courses on garden history and design.

There is an imaginative ordering of the garden so that the visitor who strolls along its fine gravel walks will truly experience a voyage through botanical time.

I began with the herb garden, for the Garden was founded by the Society of Apothecaries. Their use for herbs was medicinal, and the survival of the word 'physic' expresses this but at the same time is misleading, for in its period the Garden embraced the wider concept of a botanic garden of the kind already established in Italy at Padua or in the Netherlands at Leiden. And that we can see here vividly in the disposal of the plants like a Renaissance botanical encyclopedia overlaid with the new science of the seventeenth century. We witness in tangible form that leap of the human mind which wished to order and codify God's creation the more to marvel at it. So the beds are arranged in orderly little rectangles and the plants within them set in a stately progression of types like some vast visual card index. Early museums and zoos worked from the same thought premise – which brings one squarely to Sir Hans Sloane, who bought the Manor of Chelsea, including the Physic Garden, in 1712.

Sloane's surname more immediately evokes in our own day the 'ranger' in a Hermès headscarf than the man whose full-size statue by Rysbrack presides over the Garden. The original is in the British Museum, and what we now see is a resin copy to which the missing nose and foot have been obligingly restored. Sloane's enormous collections were the origin of both the British and Natural History Museums. It is important to see the Garden as an aspect of those collections, for he specified that fifty specimens of plants grown in the garden should pressed annually and kept there. They survive to this day, a mine of information on eighteenth-century plants.

Sloane saw to it also that the great botanical horticulturist Philip Miller was appointed as gardener, the most famous of a succession which included William Forsythe, of forsythia fame. An historic garden is laid out to commemorate Miller and his most famous plants, including cotton, the seeds of which were sent to Georgia.

The historical and botanical sides are fascinating, but belie the enormous impact that the Garden has on the ordinary visitor who penetrates the gate. It is not that large an area, but its somewhat irregular layout into quarters makes it seem larger than it really is.

It is also crammed with thousands of plants, just one of each, arranged for and by the botanist and certainly not by or for the designer. The result is unexpectedly beguiling. One keeps on coming across the oddest juxtapositions. A small rectangular canal filled with lilies and marsh marigolds is bordered by an extraordinary bed which contains nothing but varieties of salvia from the four corners of the globe: the Mediterranean, Russia, Rumania, Morocco, Kenya, California. The beautiful silver furry grey leaves of *Salvia argentea* arise for example, next to her coarse-leaved sister, *S. bucharia* (now named *S. pratensis* ssp. *dumetorum*).

Equally strange in terms of location is the rockery, which

is plonked down in one of the spandrels close to the statue of Sloane. There is a little oval pond on the top of it, where two ducks snoozed in the sun when I was there. It is the earliest rock garden, 1772 in date, and objectively as awful as some of its lineal descendants in suburban gardens today. This pile of stones from the Tower of London, mingled with some brought back from Mount Hecla by the eighteenth-century naturalist Sir Joseph Banks, is abundant evidence, if any is needed, that bad taste gardening existed also in the past. But there it is, a true curiosity.

Everything is labelled – even the trees, which often wear their labels like a kind of pendant to a necklace. I stood inside a glorious weeping beech, its branches and leaves dappled by sun trailing like the skirts of a crinoline almost to the ground. I marvelled at the *Catalpa bignonioides*, yet to leaf, and the gnarled black mulberry, its trunk worthy of being drawn by Arthur Rackham.

So much beauty and atmosphere aligned to so much information and history. Just the fact of this patch of cultivated earth surviving as an oasis of calm while everything else around it arose and fell over three centuries is extraordinary in itself.

COURANCES

One of the garden visits which has given me most pleasure was to Courances, the great château garden not so far from Paris, belonging to the Ganay family. The sky was a clear blue and sun touched leaves which were just on the turn to ochre and russet. This was one of those rare revelatory mornings which remind the gardener how important the quality of light is to a garden's atmosphere, for it fell at Courances that morning through the trees as though angels would descend along its path. Magic filled the air in this most magical of French classic gardens.

What is Courances and why should that be so? In my experience Courances is unique among the great French formal gardens for it does not overwhelm. The scale of the majority is such that the visitor is reduced to being an ant, a mere cipher. And no doubt that was part of their intent, created as they were in ages of absolutism and aristocracy. Versailles leaves one obliterated it is so gargantuan. Courances uses the same formula but retains a humanity. At every step one warms to it.

What we see today is a nineteenth-century re-creation of a seventeenth-century garden by the great father-and-son team of Henri and Achille Duchêne, who were responsible also for restoring some of the greatest of the creations of Louis XIV's gardener, André Le Nôtre, at Vaux le Vicomte and Versailles, both within striking distance of Courances. They went on later to create a series of French-style gardens in the United States and we can see their work in a final flurry of aristocratic profligacy in the water parterre at Blenheim Palace, near Oxford, laid out in the 1920s. That garden style works from the premise of mathematical modules on a grid system whose focal point is the residence, which fans out from that in a stately progression from parterres to fountains and ponds, by way of geometrical plantings of trees and shrubs and radiating *allées* which subjugate the landscape beyond. It is rigorous and exact, and a pure expression – in garden terms – of the thinking of the great seventeenth-century philosopher René Descartes.

Here it all is at Courances with virtually not a flower in sight (which I know for the British is a killer), a masterly essay in green geometry. It opens with the fanfare of a double *allée* of plane trees lining canals whose perspective culminates in the brick and stone château glimpsed through ironwork *clair voyée* grills and gates. Then comes a moat whose water is crystalline. It is the clear translucent nature of the rushing waters gushing into its ponds and canals from huge dolphin heads which leaves one of the most imperishable impressions. It is of course one thing to be lucky enough to have all that water but it is quite another to know how to handle it. Both château and sky are reflected in a large pond in false perspective encompassed by greensward, held in by a box hedge interspersed with statues, with soaring chestnut, pine and plane trees behind. This in its turn has *allées* off it, leading to more canals and ponds. Words are inadequate to convey the sense of total harmony which this simple combination of water, trees, grass and statuary gives.

Courances today is maintained by just two gardeners coping with 150 acres. The main battle is the grass and they are experimenting with chemicals to slow down its growth. The magnificent box parterre at the rear of the château, which demands cutting twice a year looks tired and work is in hand to revive it. About a century old, the trees too are beginning to call for attention. But part of the charm and accessibility of the garden lies in a lingering sense of romantic impinging decay.

When it was laid out it was one of a series which

proclaimed that the French had rediscovered their own garden heritage, having been taken over by *le jardin anglais* since the late eighteenth century, a supremacy which was maintained throughout the Victorian period. In 1911 Lucien Corpechet could write with renewed pride in his *Parcs et Jardins de France*: 'The French have been the only people in the world to understand this art of gardens, as Le Nôtre understood it . . . They are gardens of intelligence.' Ah yes, but of romance too, at least in the case of Courances.

The Royal Botanic Gardens,

Madrid

The Spaniards whom we asked about Madrid's Royal Botanic Garden were somewhat dismissive of it. They should not have been, for it is quite outstanding. Its situation alone is extraordinary, as though the Chelsea Physic Garden had been lifted and relocated next to the National Gallery in Trafalgar Square. The Royal Botanic Garden is next to the Prado, so that there is no excuse for arguing that it is off the tourist beat. The entrance, a handsome late eighteenth-century one in the neo-classical style by the court architect Juan de Villanueva, is from the Plaza de Murillo. It is to one side of the gardens, which are laid out in a triple series of ascending terraces that culminate in what was once a huge greenhouse by the same man. The royal entrance, again designed by Villanueva, is on the central axis along the Paseo del Prado and it is from there that the visitor gains the full impact of what was even for that date an old-fashioned symmetrical layout.

Having raised my hands in despair at so many run-down and dilapidated botanic gardens I was quite unprepared for the sight which greeted me. Everything was neat and in order. The paths were sanded and raked, weed free, and the gardeners, in smart green dungarees, were busy watering the plants, clipping the hedges or tending the beds. This is a green paradise in which to walk on even the hottest day, for every path is canopied by luxuriant trees and the intersection of each garden with the next is marked by a small fountain. Pictures of the garden before its present restoration was undertaken in 1974 provide some index of a remarkable achievement. The seven-year restoration programme transformed what had become a desolate wilderness into one of the city's handsomest open spaces.

What the visitor sees is a compromise which preserves elements from two quite distinct phases in the garden's history. Although it was founded in 1756, late in European terms, it only came to its present site twenty-five years later. The garden now covers twenty acres and the first two of its terraces have been restored to the series of large geometrically patterned squares from a plan of 1786 while the third, the uppermost, follows a remodelling from the 1850s. The result cannot be described as anything other than an utter delight, giving pleasure both to the keenest plantsperson as well as to the more design-oriented.

The lower terrace gardens are edged with box and within them, planted seemingly pell-mell, are stunning specimen trees, both deciduous and evergreen, which soften any rigidity. Everything is clearly and meticulously labelled and there are comfortable stone benches and wooden seats on which to sit. The second terrace is laid out in the classic taxonomic terms usual for a botanic garden. In the lower terrace gardens, however, are gathered together, for example, plants endemic to the Iberian peninsula, such as *Salvia candelabrum*, *Cytisus striatus*, *Genista hispanica* and *Centaurea clementei*. A little way on there are gardens full of vegetables of the kind glimpsed in the Spanish still life paintings in the nearby Prado: cabbages, corn, pimentos and potatoes. In the paintings are some trained over bamboo frames constructed like tents, often the earth is banked up in a particular manner to hold in water.

What is overwhelming is to take in the plants which came to Europe via the vast Spanish Empire in the New World. A dazzling display of varieties of dahlias from Mexico caught my eye, including a twelve-foot high *Dahlia excelsa*. The garden is a monument to the explosion in botanical studies in Spain during the period of the Enlightenment. This was epitomised by the publication in 1762 of a book by the garden's first director, Joseph Quer: *Flora Espanola*, the first systematic listing of the country's native flora, which followed the new system of classification of Linnaeus. His bust arises from an oval pond decked with waterlilies outside the greenhouse. The garden's first botanic expedition in 1777 lasted no less than a decade. It was the most enterprising and extensive of its time, bringing back to Europe from Peru and Chile the greatest variety of plants ever seen. Other expeditions followed, importing plants such as daturas, sandalwood, indigo, rosewood, rubber plants and the coca plant from which cocaine is derived.

The Royal Botanic Garden in Madrid was to experience

untold ups and downs in its fortunes, victim of Spain's turbulent history, which reads like one long string of devastation running from the battles fought during the Napoleonic period down to the Spanish civil war of our own century. The contrast with the tranquil story of England's Kew Gardens could not be more dramatic. For any visitor who wants refreshment of the spirits after the marble halls of the Prado here is a treat indeed, just a few steps away.

THE BOBOLI GARDENS, FLORENCE

We go to Florence once a year, usually in the last week of February or the first one of March when the city is virtually devoid of tourists, bar the insatiable Japanese, and one can benefit from the winter hotel rates. Even at that time of year more often than not one hits some days of brilliant sunshine and blue skies, and even if we don't we still always make our way on our annual pilgrimage across the Ponte Vecchio. For decades, when I was younger, it was always to soldier through the cavernous gilded galleries of the Pitti Palace; but now we head straight for the *anfiteatro* at the back of the building which forms the first great set piece of the Boboli Gardens. These are some of the greatest of surviving Renaissance gardens, and predate those of the Villa Lante at Bagnaia and the Villa d'Este at Tivoli. And yet I am always struck by how few people seem to visit the Boboli Gardens, let alone grasp their full wonder. They are not, I admit, for the sedentary, for some of their choicest beauties demand an uphill striding gait calling for the attributes of a mountain goat. But they are well worth the effort.

The news that a comprehensive strategy for their restoration and conservation is under way could not be more welcome. One of the reasons that they are under-appreciated by British visitors is that we've been spoilt. To anyone used to the high maintenance levels of the average National Trust garden, let alone to anyone with a mind fixed with the definition that a garden equals a Jekyllesque herbaceous border, the Boboli inevitably look shabby and unloved with their overgrown hedges, broken statuary, ailing trees, disintegrating garden buildings, stagnant water and fountains which barely work. Add to that their latter-day transformation into a municipal park and you have all the off-putting ingredients which can obscure the eye from drinking in one of the world's greatest garden experiences.

When John Evelyn visited the Boboli Gardens in 1644 he was transported: 'The Garden is full of all Variety, hills, dales, rocks, Groves, aviaries, viviaries, fountaines ... & whatsoever may render such a Paradise delightfull ...' For those who want to savour what the paradise was once like I recommend heading to the gardens' furthest point towards the Porta Romana. There sits what I hold to be one of garden-making's greatest compositions, the Isolotto, a huge oval enclosure delineated by massive walls of clipped evergreen holm oak and laurel holding in a large oval pond with an island in the centre. On the island there is a box parterre filled in summer with lemon trees in vast terracotta pots and in the middle arises the sculptor Giambologna's ravishing *Fountain of the Ocean*. But it's the articulation of the balustrading, the soaring columns which herald the two bridges over to the island, the *putti* and other figures which arise from the surrounding waters, not to mention the water-spouting harpies, which never cease to amaze. Perfection of proportion, sinuous elegance, movement yet calm are all here responding to the light of a Tuscan sky. It's a little sad today, I know, but think what restoration could do! Just to see all the water jetting as of old would be a revelation.

The Boboli Gardens were laid out in the 1550s as symbols of the new-found magnificence of the Medici grand dukes. The restoration scheme will need to take into consideration several layers over the centuries, five at least. There's the one from the 1550s and '60s, a garden of the earliest Renaissance kind, geometric with a central axis and everything symmetrical. Then there's the fantastic late sixteenth-century overlay, when optimistic harmony had been replaced by an unease and fear of the irrationality of nature as expressed in the Grotto Grande, for example, with its fantastic evocation, through illusionistic painting, stucco, pebbles, sculpture, vegetation and trickling water, of a cave about to collapse on the visitor. Next comes the seventeenth century, with its outdoor *anfiteatro*, already restored, and the thrust westwards with the splendid statue-lined axial avenue, the Viottolone, of ilex, laurel and cypress. Add to that the contribution of the Enlightenment and a flirtation with the *giardino Inglese* and there are all the ingredients of a conservationist's nightmare. Tip in the problems of funding and the labyrinthine ways of Italian cultural bureaucracy, no single person having absolute control, and anything could happen. What will go and what will stay? It will be intriguing to watch. But in the meantime step out and explore these gardens and give Raphael and Titian a miss.

PLÄS BRONDANW

A notice read that the garden was open, adding, trustingly, that I should put £1.50 in the box secured to its reverse. I did so, having first swung open the huge wrought-iron gate painted in a shade of greenish turquoise which acts almost as signature to the work of Sir Clough Williams-Ellis. The Italianate village he designed near by, Portmeirion, is filled with it and so is his garden at the old family home called Pläs Brondanw, a somewhat gaunt Welsh stone gentry house superbly sited a few miles away. To the east it is backed by a rising wooded hillside, the garden aspect looking west across Traeth Mawr towards a breathtaking backdrop of the mountains of Snowdonia. He was given the house in 1902 when he was just nineteen. Its garden was to be his life's work, a long one, for he died aged ninety-five in 1978.

I once met this remarkable man at a Royal Academy dinner. He was a gracious, somewhat dandified Edwardian figure, then into his final decade, but it wasn't until much later that he was to enter my gardening pantheon. Here was a soul-mate, someone who wanted to make a great garden with no cash. What he wrote in his autobiography rings every bell: 'It was for its sake that I worked and stinted, for its sake that I chiefly hoped to prosper. A cheque for ten pounds would come in and I would order yew hedging to that extent, a cheque for twenty and I would pave a further piece.' Oh, how I know the feeling!

So I made the visit with a sense of pilgrimage, but I never go to a garden, great or small, without wanting to learn, to analyse its points of success or failure. This is an architect's garden, one laid out by someone who had fallen in love with the great gardens of Renaissance Italy in the era of Edith Wharton and Cecil Pinsent, creator of I Tatti. And yet to my eye its astounding yew enclosures and topiary carry with them more than an echo of that prototype 'olde world' English garden, Levens Hall in Westmorland. Being an architect's garden means that it is not a plantsman's paradise; it draws instead on the deep satisfaction to be had from handsome green walls and bastions of yew, box and beech, flights of stone steps, water, both moving and still, paths of slate, the use of *clair voyée* effects, changes of level and a motley of statuary. Like our garden, The Laskett, it's grandeur on the cheap.

Unlike ours, however, its articulation is decided by the landscape in which it sits, with vistas and cross-axes leading the eye to one or other distant peak. There is something to be learnt from the wonderful *frisson* experienced from contemplating internal clipped formality silhouetted against the external wild. There is even more to be learned from this garden about the importance of skyline. Why do so few of our garden designers ever look upward? I recall seeing, not so long ago, one newly laid-out garden by one of our famous lady gardeners. It was ravishing until one lifted one's eyes on the main vista which culminated in the field beyond with an electric junction box. Her eyes had been firmly clamped down on to the earth at her feet. Clough reminds us of the importance of very strong architectural verticals, the excitement of seeing something soaring into the heavens. He places urns on piers fifteen or twenty feet high so that they sing out against the sky. His leitmotif is the Irish yew, his substitute for the tender Italian cypress, tied in and clipped into narrow columns placed as exclamation marks in the composition. That I'm already copying. It's an effect he used for Ottoline Morrell's flower garden at Garsington, Oxfordshire, in 1915, a grid of box-edged rectangles, with narrow pyramids of Irish yew in the corners and the beds filled with seasonal flowers. Those one looks for in vain at Pläs Brondanw, though to be fair Clough is good on practicalities: the siting of compost heaps and an enclosure for hardwood cuttings are carefully thought through.

Clough, one knows from Portmeirion, was never afraid of colour. The buildings are colour-washed ochre, terracotta, primrose, a dusky blue. His beloved greeny-turquoise with touches of ochre, in which the ironwork in the garden, added over the years, is painted, also recurs on the house. How many people ever think of linking house and garden colour-wise? He reminds any gardener that colour is not only flowers. It is what comes out of the paint pot and the possibilities for the imaginative are limitless. The entire of The Laskett garden is held together by washes of cinnamon and a blue which we first saw in Russia, together with touches of gilding. On a brilliant winter's day, especially under snow, the effect is entrancing. We forget that in the centuries before the pollution of the Industrial Revolution technicolour iron and carpentry work reigned in the garden.

He also reminds us how to incorporate what is there already into a formal scheme. An ancient ilex just to one side of the central vista from the house is encircled by an oval of balustrading drawing it graciously into the composition. Pläs Brondanw is a garden which, if it were less remotely sited, would be far more celebrated than it is.

GARDENS NEW

H aving a perspective over half a century and a keen sense of history, I can see already the ebbs and flows of those decades falling into place in terms of garden style. The four gardens here to some extent etch in that story. After 1945 the story of garden design was largely one of survival tactics and contraction, and it was not until the 1970s that it was possible even to think of private gardening in the grand manner again. That revival was made possible by modern mechanical aids and then, in the 1980s, by a reversal of taxation policy together with a reawakening to gardening as an expression of personal taste. The 1970s, on account of social turbulence, had triggered a turning back, a realisation of what had been lost, summed up in that word which has now become almost a liability, heritage. Hatfield Old Palace, in Hertfordshire, is a pure expression of that reaching back to the past.

Not only was garden conservation and restoration born, there was also a flurry of Jekyllesque Arts and Crafts gardens and a cornucopia of knots and parterres, heralds of a return to formality. Our own garden, The Laskett, was laid out during this period and, with its emphasis on vista, topiary and ornament, reflects all those impulses towards nostalgia and historicism. What it also demonstrates is that it was possible to plant quite an elaborate garden in the grand manner with not much cash or labour. Those, however, who have an abundance of both can go the whole hog. That opportunity was the allure, for me, of designing an Italianate garden for Elton John, a *coup de théâtre* of a kind not seen, I think, since Harold Peto's creations in the Edwardian age. John's garden reflects accurately that it is to pop that panache and panoply, once the prerogative of dynasties, has migrated.

Ian Hamilton Finlay, at Little Sparta, sternly calls us to tread another path, one that has profoundly influenced me, drawing gardening back from the precipice of vacuity. We need a reminder that the greatest gardens are those which exercise not just the primary senses but also the intricacies of the educated intellect.

HATFIELD OLD PALACE:
THE MARCHIONESS OF SALISBURY

I must have first visited Hatfield House in about 1950 when, as a schoolboy of 15, with a consuming passion for the first Elizabeth, I naturally made my way to the great house crammed with pictures and relics of her age. The house itself was rebuilt after her death by her last minister, Robert Cecil, but close by it stands the old palace in which the young princess spent much of her time during her sister Mary's reign. The latter is a building of soft rose-red brick, now the only remaining side of what had once been a courtyard house, the missing ones being marked by banks rising steeply on three sides enclosing a rectangular area of grass. This always looked forlorn and unloved, as though it was awaiting someone to wave a wand and create a spectacle worthy of such a magnificent history.

That moment came when the present Marchioness of Salisbury, whom I once described as this country's greatest gardener, laid out a knot garden in the vacant quadrangle in 1981. At this point I really must declare my hand, for the reader will suspect that, as I am an historian by profession, my obsession would be the re-creation in detail of a garden from the past. That, I know, can be done and done successfully, but the result is often sterile and more often just plain wrong. What is more interesting is when someone reinterprets an idiom from the past and gives it new life in contemporary garden terms. And that is precisely what this new knot garden does, for although it happens to be sited in a grand historical setting, the format is adaptable to the tiniest of gardens.

Lady Salisbury might be said to have pioneered the revival of this type of garden single-handed. There were earlier attempts to re-create them, after the First World War at Shakespeare's birthplace in Stratford-upon-Avon, Warwickshire, and at Hampton Court. Both are still there and well worth a visit. But it is only in the last twenty years that we have seen a steady stream of them – all designed by Lady Salisbury – from Crichel and Cranborne Manor in Dorset to the Tradescant Trust's garden at St Mary's Lambeth in London, and the one planted for the Prince of Wales at Highgrove, Gloucestershire, in which the letters C and D appear entwined.

Knot gardens needs to be looked down on, for their essence is pattern created by clipped dwarf hedges. At Hatfield, therefore, the site is ideal, for the public can look at it precisely as it would have been viewed in its own day by strolling along a terrace raised around its sides.

In the words of the Elizabethans, this garden is 'cast into quarters' and divided by tiny paths of brick with a central circular fountain as its focal point. Four smaller rectangular beds are at the edges but the main garden consists of four knots, each of a different pattern. The old garden books copied each other when it came to designs for knots, with the result that they remained virtually unchanged for a century. The designs were given fancy names such as Trefoil, Cinquefoil, Crossbow, Diamond and the Fret. Hatfield draws on these, simplifying and not copying them. The original designs are so intricate that it defies belief that anyone ever did plant them, let alone maintain them, composed as they were of tiny clipped hedges of rosemary, thyme or cotton lavender. Here all the hedges are of dwarf box, which gives year-round pleasure. In one quarter there is a tiny maze but the others are made up of combinations of diamonds, squares, ovals and circles. The corners are marked by sentinels of box clipped into cones and there are further set pieces of topiary, in particular a row of gold-edged, standard hollies clipped into multi-tiered cakestands which arise beneath the old palace walls.

Here, the historical side ends: the beds within explode with a planting of a variety and richness unknown to Tudor England. There is nothing dull or flat about this knot garden. Here height is added by a luxuriant planting of old roses: *Rosa* 'Quatre Saisons', *R. gallica* var. *officinalis* and *R. g.* 'Versicolor' and *R.* × *centifolia*. Each of them is carefully labelled, as indeed is every single other plant which carpets a soil rich in leaf mould and with never a weed in sight. The planting is thick and random with a masterful, calculated dishevelment. Here we see a typical manifestation within the tradition of Gertrude Jekyll in which a formal structure is offset by a planting in the cottage idiom. Last time I was there, in May, I caught the tail end of the spring: primulas, jonquils, hellebores, hyacinths, narcissi and tulips, many of rare varieties. One I noted, called after Sir Joseph Paxton, the designer of the Crystal Palace, had petals of the darkest plum streaked with gold. The flowers of summer were yet to come, although the roses had already put forth their leaves and the grey-leaved lychnis and the peonies were pushing upwards. The predominant yellows, creams and whites of spring would shortly be giving way to the multiplicity of shades of pink typical of June.

In the past, gardens were enclosed by hedges, often of hawthorn. We are so used to seeing this for hedgerows that it is easy to forget that it can also be used for formal hedging, although it requires cutting more than once during the growing season. At Hatfield it encloses the entire garden, in places rising in height to provide a back wall for a simple arbour, where seats of wooden slats sit underneath a wood and wire arch, bearing honeysuckle to scent the air. No seat in this garden is without a scented plant near by, whether it is the astringent aroma of cotton lavender, the heady sweetness of old-fashioned lavender or spikes of rosemary leaves to press between the fingers.

I suppose if I had to encapsulate the extraordinary spell cast by this garden it would be its utter Englishness. These early gardens always seem to have had a domestic quality to their scale. You went to the same man whether you wanted a pattern for your knot garden or one to embroider on a sleeve or cushion cover. That, to me, captures the essence of the formula, which has a delicacy and lightness of touch to it. It is typically English in its concern with decoration and two-dimensional pattern, and there is no hint of that off-putting, overwhelming formality which is the bane of grand French gardens. I feel comfortably at home here as I gaze down and respond to the feeling of total delight which it gives to me as I watch the pattern of sun and shadow move across it.

THE LASKETT: OUR OWN GARDEN

I always wish creators of gardens had written more. Few do, and we are the poorer for it, as nothing is more fascinating than learning from the pen of the only begetter. Nor do many gardeners have any archival sense. One is horrified by the paucity, in the era of the camera, of visual evidence, for example, of those two horticultural war-horses of our age, Hidcote Manor, in Gloucestershire and Sissinghurst Castle, Kent. Well, no one need fear that in the case of our own garden, should it join the ranks of the survivors. From the moment of its inception every bill has been kept, every design and thousands of photographs too, besides, in recent years, garden diaries. In addition, through over fifty volumes of scrapbooks we can trace the story of The Laskett garden from field to folly. But even that is not enough; fascinating though visual and archival evidence may be, it only tells When and How, evading that most compelling question of them all, Why.

But let me begin at the beginning – with the house itself. The Laskett, a word in Herefordshire dialect meaning a strip of land outside the parish, lies on the fringes of the village of Much Birch, midway between Ross-on-Wye and Hereford. As my wife, Julia Trevelyan Oman, always says, it is building rather than architecture, a pink sandstone box from the

1820s evoking the modesty of a rectory in a novel by Jane Austen. That a huge garden might be made was certainly never part of our plans at the outset, as is reflected in the fact that no one who was going to make a large formal garden would ever have chosen a house sited, as ours is, in the corner of a three-and-a-half-acre triangle of land, thus eliminating any possibility of the classic progression through parterres, bosquets and walks radiating from and related to the house. But in the long run that deficiency has been found to have its advantages. The first is the one of surprise: nobody visiting the garden for the first time can ever guess at the spectacle that suddenly unfolds as they cross the drive past a fountain and through a slip in the beech hedge. Turning sharply left they see a great vista falling away into the distance, through three gardens, towards glimpses of a pleached lime avenue. That is where the garden proper begins. To a sense of surprise I would add the opportunity to indulge in certain grand effects which, if sited in proximity to the house, would have appeared too pretentious and out of place. The ten-foot-high column topped by a golden ball, the nine-foot-high Shakespeare Urn (commemorating the award to me in 1980 of the FVS Foundation of Hamburg's Shakespeare Prize) and the small classical Victoria & Albert Museum temple (built in memory of my years there from 1974 to 1987), which make up the eye-catchers at the ends of the grandest vistas, are so far from the house that they have taken on the character of total fantasies in an imaginary landscape.

Both house and garden are south-facing and the land gently slopes away, presenting us at the outset with few level surfaces except that of the site of an Edwardian lawn-tennis court. And that was where we started, for it was in the field attached to the house let to a farmer as pasture for his cows. His decision in 1974 that he did not want it any longer set us on our way. Together we stood and looked at the three-foot-high grass and realised that something had to be done; and it was on the flat surface of the court, when mowing had revealed the fine turf beneath the grass, that we began, in December in that year, to plant one of our first yew hedges, around what was to be the Pierpont Morgan Rose Garden (named for the lectures I gave in the Pierpoint Morgan Library in 1974). At the time I felt the lack of flat terrain a tremendous disadvantage, but now I realise our good fortune, as changes in level, as every true gardener knows, form some of the most thrilling experiences. That only dawned much later, when we learnt that built structure could be added as and when it could be afforded. So, piecemeal over the years the flights of steps and paving came, necessitating only a realignment of hedges, letting one side grow up to re-establish levels within the composition.

But what about the soil? It is light and sandy, reddish in colour, too quick-draining, and calling for constant compost and mulch to keep the moisture in. It tolerates rhododendrons and azaleas but they cannot be said exactly to thrive. Willows won't grow, and all except the most common of prunus are fated. Putting those black marks aside, practically everything else does pretty well and some things spectacularly so. Yew hedging, one of my great loves, shoots up at the rate of a foot to eighteen inches a year and, as most of the garden's most important rooms are formed of it, this has proved a great blessing. Sprigs two feet high become eight-foot walls in a decade. And, of course,

Herefordshire being the cider county, malus flourish, and my wife's passion has become old apple trees and the decorative crabs, of which altogether she has some hundred or so. This soil is also an ideal one in which to grow grey foliage plants but, as they are tender, one has to protect them from the wind. Wind, in fact, even more than rabbits and moles, was to be and still is our greatest enemy, horrendous gales blowing from the Black Mountains felling branches, even whole trees. The garden's climatic history has included the great drought of 1976 and the bitter winters of the early 1980s; in one of those we suffered from 24°F of frost which wiped out much, including a fifteen-foot-high avenue of *Nothofagus procera*. To these minuses we can add that on arrival we had to take down seven elm trees, and that the chestnut avenue up the drive promptly died, followed a few years later by a superb beech and a turkey oak. None the less, an ever-open cheque-book and a succession of tree surgeons have ensured that the mighty cedar of Lebanon which holds the whole house in its arms still presides over the front lawn.

But I have yet to explain what led us to do it, apart from the necessity of filling the field with something. My first year as Director of the Victoria & Albert Museum was 1974. It was the period of the fall of the Heath government, the oil crisis, and industrial and social unrest. The feeling of uncertainty about the future of things was encapsulated in the first exhibition I rushed into the museum, 'The Destruction of the Country House'. This brought home to the public, by using the museum as polemic, the full horror of what we had lost in this century, in terms not only of houses but of gardens too, and went on to spell out the dangers ahead. It was a time of deep gloom, and I clearly remember that the act of planting our garden was a deliberate and defiant one. In spite of it all I believed with a great passion that that most English of all art forms, the classic country house garden, would go on. With no money, little labour, but much love and not a little vision, we would make one. We would plant our yews in this dark hour and hold fast in the knowledge that they would grow and we would live to clip them into pinnacles and peacocks, and so it has proved. But that could not be foreseen amid the turbulence of the second half of the 1970s.

By 1975 we had a plan; in fact, I still have what I drew in the summer of that year. Its design emerged out of what I loved and knew best. There was never any question but that the garden was to be formal. I was mesmerised by the country house views in Kip's *Nouveau Théâtre de la Grande Bretagne* (published later in 1716 and 1724), recording late Stuart gardens with their stately avenues, patterned planting and enclosures, a form of gardening that gave architecture and articulation purely through the ordered siting of trees and shrubs. Next for inspiration came the photographs by Charles Latham in *Gardens Old and New* (1910), that set of volumes which records the country house gardens of Edwardian England on the eve of the Deluge of 1914. Constantly I would go for walks in those photographs looking for ideas for The Laskett – ideas, that is, that we could afford. Then there were real gardens. Hidcote Manor, of course, first visited by us on a chill winter's day with the late Lady Hartwell. Pamela's husband, Michael, has made a marvellous garden of this kind at Oving, which was another inspiration because it consisted purely of trees and shrubs held together by sculptural ornament. Two other friends provided further impulses, Sir Cecil Beaton and John Fowler. Cecil was the first person ever to walk me round a garden, which he regularly did at his garden at Reddish House in Broadchalke, Wiltshire. This seemingly simple act, like so many in one's life, was seminal in opening up to me the very idea that one could actually make a garden at all. Although Beaton's garden was beautiful, its design did not affect me as much as John Fowler's miraculous creation at King John's Hunting Lodge at Odiham. This is the most perfectly articulated small garden I have ever seen. It excited me above all to the effects which could be achieved by training. Features such as the stilt hedges and the use of clipped box for formal accents stayed imprinted on my mind.

The trouble is that, almost twenty years on, so many other influences have come tumbling in. Italy certainly, which I first fell in love with in 1955, but the gardens only came in the 1970s. The Villa Lante and the Villa Farnese haunted me; it was fifteen years before we could afford to grace the first grand vista with steps, balustrading and a distant temple, but such artefacts were always in my mind's eye from the very beginning. Het Loo in Holland constantly seized my imagination during the 1980s, with the result that more box and ground pattern began to spring up everywhere. The Yew Garden near the house, where I planted my first minute box parterre, suddenly exploded in size. A box and gravel parterre with our initials entwined at its centre was laid out on the far side of the garden and, in front of the house, a design from Gervase Markham's *The English Husbandman* (1613) was planted, adding a carpet at the feet of the statue of Flora that already stood there.

The main layout of the garden has never really radically

changed over two decades, but it has been developed and refined enormously. This is the result not only of having seen new things, but also of having made terrible mistakes, or of finding that a particular scheme was either unmaintainable or simply didn't work. Garden ornaments in particular have frequently migrated before finding their final resting-place. With ornament I have no snobbery, and ours is a happy mishmash of old and new – in fact whatever I think I can get away with at a distance. The Associates of the Victoria & Albert Museum presented me with what was then our only new artefact as a farewell present, a plaque by Simon Verity which is like a medal, in which my profile is sandwiched between that of the Queen and the Prince Consort.

The achievement of any garden must be considered in relation to the commitment in terms of both time and labour. Contrary to general belief, formality and size are marvellous concealers of untidiness and lack of finish. Through the fourteen years that I directed the museum, I was never able to give the garden the input it demanded. But it was during these very years that its vital infrastructure of shrubberies, hedges and screens grew, making the later elaboration possible. All of this was achieved by just the two of us, plus the equivalent of an untrained gardener one day a week. We had to accept a relaxed philosophy over what got done and what had to be left. If the weeds sprang and the branches got entangled, we merely looked at those areas through romantic eyes. Now we have a gardener for three days a week, and cannot contain our excitement as to what we hope to achieve in this new era.

Inevitably, until recently plants have had to take something of a back seat. One of the great joys of this present phase is to see that position being slowly reversed. In 1988 I planted a Flower Garden: it is rather Reptonesque in shape, but for the first time I have been able to indulge in and learn about herbaceous borders, and also to start thinking more intensively about the seasonal sequences.

The Silver Jubilee Garden, once only at its apogee in a froth of white and lilac in June, now has an autumnal finale of Michaelmas daisies coinciding with the second flush of the 'Iceberg' roses. Julia has turned her hand to the spring planting, which now unfolds in a complex rhythm which begins in January and lasts until the close of May. Flora in her glade is never without a bloom at her feet from the earliest snowdrops, through scillas, chionodoxas, tiny daffodils, fritillaries and aconites. The formal beds are planted in succession to achieve a display of tulips and hyacinths over as long a period as possible. The stunning great *allée* of daffodils along the pleached lime avenue is succeeded by purple alliums amid cow parsley, like a Sisley painting. The winding walk, the Serpentine, is thick with ribbons of 'White Lion' daffodils, which fade as the Flower Garden springs to life. Recent new planting at the boundaries is aimed at giving glorious sunset-coloured foliage to enliven the autumn skyline.

The Laskett is an autobiographical garden, for our life together is etched into its many compartments. They have to be called something and often they were constructed with money made through a book or a theatrical production. It must sound eccentric to visitors as they are guided along the pleached lime avenue, Elizabeth Tudor (my wife and I did a little book on her in 1972), or sit in the Ashton Arbour of clipped yew (named to recall Sir Frederick, two of whose ballets Julia designed), looking towards a tableau of topiary peacocks set, as it were, on a stage which we call Covent Garden (where Julia also designed three operas). It is all a bit arbitrary and sometimes, in the case of the statuary, just plain dotty. A recumbent stag will be christened Franco because of a book I wrote for the brilliant Italian publisher Franco Maria Ricci, or a classical female bust Lucia because we were in an E.F. Benson phase.

But it does mean that every space in the garden is thick with association and memories of a life together and of our mutual creativity. Of course, it is rich beyond that with other memories, above all of people. A sundial from Cecil Beaton's garden stands at the centre of the garden we planted in honour of the Queen's Silver Jubilee in 1977. That to me symbolises a precious friendship, for I often stayed with him and the exhibition of his portrait photographs at the National Portrait Gallery in 1968 lit the blue touch-paper of my career. Julia's family, the Omans, is recalled by an urn at the centre of the Rose Garden which came from the house of her aunt, the writer Carola Oman, at Bride Hall in Hertfordshire. A pinnacle from All Souls and a lion from the Houses of Parliament are evidence of her distinguished grandfather, Sir Charles Oman, the historian and MP for the University of Oxford. These came from Frewin Hall where he lived, as also did a descendant of a quince tree which now flourishes at The Laskett, and the agapanthus which have been multiplied and passed down through the family for almost a century. Every year we look forward to that heavenly blue bursting upon us on the terrace.

I have not yet mentioned either the orchard or the vegetable garden, which are my wife's domain. We have over sixty varieties of apple trees, going back to the twelfth century, all of them on dwarf rooting stock. They look beautiful in spring with their explosion of bloom and equally ravishing in autumn laden with fruits. A Finnish apple steamer bubbles away during the fruiting season, producing juice which we bottle and lay down. A second, smaller orchard contains peaches, and in a good year a tree can produce up to thirty. But it is the vegetable garden which is our real cornucopia. It makes no claim to be a decorative potager, although it has at its centre a small arched tunnel heavy with honeysuckle, *Rosa* 'Albertine' and what the friend who gave it to me calls the 'Gardener's Rose'. Spilling over amid the vegetables will be pot marigolds, nasturtiums and hardy geraniums, and herbs of every kind. Its heart is the edible produce. Joy Larkcom's oriental vegetables have given it a new dimension recently, but we also always purchase seeds in France and Italy and cast them upon the earth in hope. The fact that for ten months of the year we eat our own salad greens is some measure of the success. There are asparagus, onions, potatoes, carrots, leeks, spinach, as well as gooseberries, Jerusalem artichokes and rhubarb. Beyond this wired enclosure about a dozen compost heaps are dotted.

If you asked me what The Laskett garden was about, I might reply that it is the portrait of a marriage, the family we never had or wanted, a unique mnemonic landscape peopled with the ghosts of nearly everyone we have loved, both living and dead. It has always been conceived as an enclosed, private world, and that indeed is the key. There is no borrowed landscape. It deliberately shuts out the glory of the rolling hills of Herefordshire and remains a sealed, hermetic, magical domain of its own. And yet there is never a sense of being shut in, of claustrophobia. Instead there is just one of serene tranquillity – or as much of it as can be granted in this transitory life. For me its making has been a more extraordinary achievement than any of the books I have written or museums I have directed. To take a basket with two glasses and a bottle of wine up to the Victoria & Albert Museum temple with Julia on a summer's evening and sit contemplating the vista together in silence is happiness quantified.

WOODSIDE: SIR ELTON JOHN

The commission to design an Italian garden for Elton John came through our mutual friend, the fashion designer Gianni Versace. About a decade ago I had advised Versace, by accident, on his own garden at the Villà Fontanelle on Lake Como. On my first visit there I recall feeling sad that the once magnificent garden looked unkempt and tired – it lay like some Sleeping Beauty needing to be awakened. Sitting by the faded, dusty parterre one day, I made a series of sketches suggesting what might be done. On our next visit, Versace took us upstairs, threw open our bedroom shutters and said: 'There, Roy, is your garden.' And there, indeed, it was – the parterre had been returned to its pristine glory, but with the addition of handsome urns, while white lilies adorned the sparkling fountain at its centre. Over the years that followed I watched that garden change and grow. The parterres have multiplied and everywhere statues have sprung up: water spouts from Medusa-faced wall fountains; Neptune wields his trident against a curtain of cascading water; a river god, reclining amid ferns, presides over a sinuous floorscape of baroque scrolls etched in pebbles; and a small army of gods and goddesses now animates the hillside behind the house.

It was the sight of this newly-restored garden that made Elton John want an Italian garden too, at his house at Woodside, Old Windsor, Berkshire.

The suggestion that I should design such a garden for Elton John came from Versace and – as I have no office, nor any intention of setting up as a professional garden designer – was taken up by me solely as an act of friendship for the designer. Woodside already had a series of beautiful gardens laid out by Rosemary Verey. And that was to present me with an embarrassing situation, for the space assigned for the Italian garden was an impossible one, an area tucked away at an angle of the house with a large tree in the middle of it. Not one principle of Italian garden design, as I understood it, could have been met in that space.

Woodside is an elegant, post-Second World War essay in the neo-Georgian style in brick. Walking round the house, I confessed to seeing only one possible site for such a garden. That stretched away from the south-facing façade with its central sash and French windows flanked by wings with pretty Gothic ones. Using this as my backcloth, I saw that here an Italian garden could be made, one which fulfilled the tenets of Renaissance garden design: the interlocking of house and garden into a single composition; a central axial path together with cross axes; the use of perspective, built features, statuary and trained evergreens; and, above all, everything absolutely symmetrical.

The composition floated into my mind instantly. The French windows should open on to a balustraded terrace, which should lead on to a box parterre with statues. This would be bound by a colonnade, to secure privacy and provide a shady spot from which to look back across the garden to the house. Italian gardens are always unashamedly theatrical; this one called for a *coup de théâtre* worthy of an international star. So the colonnade should be broken in the middle to draw the eye along an avenue to a giant obelisk in the distance.

In the world of show business, everything has to be instant. I drew up the plans and elevations during Christmas 1995 and the designs were approved in February 1996, with a June deadline for a launch party on the star's return from a foreign tour. I cannot imagine that all clients are as trusting as he was, for he did not ask for a single revision. We steamed ahead and achieved what I would not have thought possible in just over three months.

I would have liked the flanking enclosing hedges to have been of yew, but the beech was there, fully grown, and to start again would have been foolish. The other compromise was the scale of the colonnade, which could have been a little higher to more advantage, but it would not have worked in relation to the scale of the house. Everything else was done just as I would have wished.

This is not a plantsman's garden. It is one which derives its pleasure from the architecture, the harmony of the geometry of the ground plan, and the use of statuary and evergreens. These elements give year-round, rather than transient delight. Much of the success of such a garden depends on the play of light. The design is of the simplest and most classic: a square quartered, making four parterre beds etched in bold box hedges. Statues of music-making satyrs, carved in Vicenza to a high standard, arise from the beds. The corners of each parterre have more verticals in the form of dark green clipped yew cones. Within each parterre, there is room for seasonal bedding-out: tulips in spring, geraniums in summer and pansies in winter. The whole is contained within paths of honey-coloured gravel.

All the architectural features are of reconstituted stone. The flanking colonnades have within them handsome stone benches on which to sit, and the flanking pairs of pillars frame busts of Roman emperors on plinths. I also introduced a feature that we have used in our own garden – colour wash in a shade of gold. This links together the whole composition and also means that even on the darkest winter's day there is a feeling of golden sunshine. There is no desire for the stonework to become discoloured and covered in moss and lichen. Its success depends on its being kept pristine, clean and sharp, with none of its composition lines obscured by climbing plants.

I was fortunate in having a wonderful team working with me who pulled out all the stops so that the garden was finished on time. When my wife and I went to see how it had settled in, it was a sun-drenched day. We entered the drawing-room, its French windows opened wide on to the new terrace and garden. Elton John stood there and we flung our arms round one another in delight. Versace had seen it shortly before he was murdered and for that I am grateful, for it now remains a monument to a friendship shared.

LITTLE SPARTA: IAN HAMILTON FINLAY

Nothing can quite prepare the visitor for the extraordinary experience of Ian Hamilton Finlay's Little Sparta, in South Lanarkshire. I had known it from photographs for years. Even then, when asked for what in my view was the most original garden created in Britain since 1945, I always never hesitated to reply, this one. A few years ago when I was leading a tour of gardens in the Scottish Lowlands we had been scheduled to go there but, in the end, the logistics in terms of distance ruled it out. Fired, however, by my eulogies, two of the party hired a car and drove hell-for-leather across country to see it. On returning they only told me how much they had hated it. That in its own way was an accolade, for such extremes of reaction to a garden are quite exceptional in our own age.

That strong emotional sense of revulsion which it had triggered signalled to me that Ian Hamilton Finlay's garden must be something quite extraordinary. When, at last, on a sun-drenched late June day I actually got there, the visit only confirmed my pre-formed judgement. To get there at all calls for the inner resources of the medieval pilgrim, for it is situated off a remote road amidst the barren moors of the southern Pentland Hills not far from Dunsyre. To reach it, one's vehicle jolts its way up a stony path across two fields, ending up in what looks like a farmyard. To the right there is an entrance gate approached by three steps with brick gate piers and, acting as a pediment, over these a large block of stone inscribed, 'A Cottage A Field A Plough'. From afar Little Sparta resembles a verdant Arcady let down from the heavens on to this windy desolate terrain.

This is a true garden experience, but so unlike the clichés which we've become accustomed to that the average visitor's first reaction is liable to be one of incomprehension and disorientation. That, in fact, reveals ignorance and our loss of the great tradition. For Little Sparta sings in the language of the classical tradition of the West, that stemming down across the centuries from the civilisations of Greece and Rome, which gives this poet and seer a tissue of allusion to reorder this particular part of the world of nature by his art, living, sculptural and verbal, to evoke bigger, more profound, intellectual resonances. In Ian Hamilton Finlay's view of things no words of condemnation can be too harsh for that modern aberration, the sculpture garden, the treatment of garden space merely as a gallery in which sculpted art is exhibited. To him that is a complete abdication of any sophisticated dialogue between the sculpture and its setting, a dialogue which is as often as not set in motion by a stray quotation or a line from a poem which sends our thoughts reeling into all kinds of directions. This view is vividly encapsulated in two lines from his *Detached Sentences on Gardening*: 'In modern gardens a bench is a thing to be sat on; in William Shenstone's garden [the Leasowes] it was a thing to be read.'

So Little Sparta is a garden of the mind. One is reminded of that fact as one wends one's way from shady grove to sparkling stream, from tranquil lake to dark grotto, all punctuated by inscriptions hung from the branches of trees, broken classical capitals flung down upon the turf or the sudden apparition, for instance, of a golden face peering upward from the water's edge. No other garden has made me so aware of the poverty of context of nearly all late twentieth-century gardens, nor made me give so much thought to my own as to its true meaning and how I can best articulate it.

This is indeed a brave and fearless creation, an invitation to inhabit a poet's thoughts. And this is precisely what some of the greatest gardens have always been about. The visitor to the garden of the Villa d'Este in the Renaissance was meant to read it and take choices as to his route, for one way led to virtue and the other vice. Stowe in the eighteenth century was a gigantic statement about the political and cultural aspirations of early Georgian England couched in terms of the manipulation of a vast aristocratic terrain. Here within the small confines of Little Sparta we see that tradition reinvented for our own age. Where else would one see a group of birch trees, the foot of each encased within the base of a classical column and inscribed with the name of one of the poet's heroes – a motley if intriguing band which includes Rousseau, Corot, Robespierre and Caspar David Friedrich. Or, to take two other examples: close to a limpid vista across water a slab bears the inscription, 'See Claude. Hear Lorraine', a tableau asking us to make a visual journey back from a garden composition inspired by one of the French painter's classical landscapes, foundations of the landscape style, to the picture itself. In much the same way the artist Dürer's monogram AD is planted firmly against turf of a kind which inspired one of the greatest of all his watercolours.

Everywhere one looks the allusions multiply. One of the most pervasive themes is the fear of power and what it can do in the hands of the absolute. Even the god Apollo is seen to be two-faced within this context. In one part of the garden there is a temple to him which has been created by incising classical columns on to a stone outbuilding, witty in itself. This presides over a calm sheet of lily-dappled water. Not far away, however, Apollo stands clasping not his traditional lyre but a machine gun. This is a garden for the educated and erudite mind and why not, in an age otherwise dedicated to the downmarket and simplistic? Hamilton Finlay cocks a much needed snook at much of contemporary garden-making. Careful consideration of his complex approach could enrich our impoverished tradition, opening doors to the extraordinary and shutting out the banal.

I found Little Sparta beguiling even in the superficial sense in which most people look at a garden, for within this small space there is a cunning orchestration of a variety of contrasting visual experiences, as one moves from light to dappled into dark, ascends uphill only to come down again, strolls along meandering paths and walks the length of a perspective vista. Changes of level and surprises as one twists and turns plus sudden views out into the landscape beyond are all part of the delights of Little Sparta, whose planting in the main is of the woodland ground-cover kind, making abundant use of lamiums, hardy geraniums and astrantia beneath wild cherry, alder, rowans and sycamores. Well might he write: 'In so far as gardening is an Art, all these may be taken under the one head, composing.'

The only blight on the poet's horizon at the moment has been his long battle with the local council. So bad has this become that Ian Hamilton Finlay has closed his garden. To be denied access to Little Sparta is to be cut off from one of the great garden inspirations of our age.

GARDEN FEATURES

When it comes to it, a garden is a collection of features that, if listed, are disparate. It is how you select those features and deploy them that makes a garden. Spying an arch, a sundial, a trellis, a container, a seat, an arbour or even a shed in a garden centre is one thing. But knowing what to do with it is quite another. That explains the explosion in the garden design profession in recent years because so many people realise that, although they are quite capable of listing the features they wish to incorporate into their garden scheme, they haven't a clue how to weld them into a coherent and pleasing composition. To achieve that calls for a visual imagination capable of making bold leaps, something which is God-given and can only to an extent be taught.

I'm lucky enough to have been endowed with that attribute and even more fortunate to be married to someone who has it in an even greater abundance. But don't think that I never make mistakes. I recall the two men who used to help us in the early days, one of whom would always say as I placed some new garden feature, 'Don't cement it down. Sir Roy is bound to want to move it.' He was right and virtually everything has moved, often several times.

All of us, however, must be haunted by those features which we know we shall never have, either for lack of space, money or labour or all three. I know that I shall never have a lake, a stream, a maze, an orangery or a green theatre. But I haven't given up on a number of other features. One I've promised my wife for her seventieth birthday is a raised rill with, overlooking it, a gothic bridge which will have a gazebo in its midst. And, even as I write, there are paths under construction and one new major feature, a tunnel of blue treillage over which medlars will be trained. I can't wait to see that next autumn, with the greeny-blue structure overlaid by the ochre, golds and oranges of the medlar leaves. A flash of sun will render it incandescent.

GREEN THEATRES

Green theatres, *teatri di verzura*, have always fascinated me, ever since I saw my first in the garden of the Villa Imperiale at Marlia, near Lucca, almost two decades ago. The green theatre there is sited on a cross axis which runs from an elegant enclosure which has in its midst a *peschiera*, a fish pond, held in by balustrading surrounded by geometrically positioned lemon trees in huge terracotta pots. Beneath a Mediterranean sun the impact is one of rapture. The beckoning vista leads to a mighty jet of water concealing the surprise to come, for beyond it, up a small flight of steps, lies hidden a complete baroque theatre in yew. In shape it is oval; and the auditorium is topped by tunnels of sculpted green with windows cut in them creating 'boxes' from which to view the stage, while below stone semi-circles form the 'stalls'. The raised stage, which is raked, has a prompt box and footlights together with side wings and an arcaded 'backcloth', all in clipped evergreen. On it now gesticulate elegant statues of figures from the *commedia dell'arte*, Harlequin and Columbine, reminding one of its long-gone use. There it has stood or rather grown since the year it was completed, 1690. There are few built equivalents. Encountering such a phenomenon in a garden one forgets what an incredible survival this tiny theatre is, once the setting for open-air recitals and entertainments in the age of Scarlatti.

Marlia isn't unique, as compulsive garden visiting soon made me aware. There seems to have been a spate of theatres planted in this area of Italy running on for a century. Not far away there's another at that fantastic garden, the Villa Garzoni at Collodi, also just outside Lucca. The garden is virtually vertical up a hillside but again on the cross axis, this time tucked away to one side, there's a tiny green theatre with the statues of Tragedy and Comedy flanking it. It is late eighteenth century in date, as indeed is another, not so easily accessible, at the Villa Bianchi-Bandinelli at Geggiano near Siena. And I've seen one more in Italy, this time going north, at the Villa Rizzardi near Verona.

Let me say at once these are not amphitheatres, another garden feature, but proscenium theatres made through terracing, planting and clipping. The idea spread northwards and others I've seen are the one at Schloss Mirabel at Salzburg and, the most spectacular, that in the great garden of the Electors of Hanover at Herrenhausen, just outside Hanover. The latter is contemporaneous with the one at Marlia, but far more flamboyant, although what we now see is a restoration, for the garden was badly damaged in the last war when the palace itself vanished. This green theatre is by far the grandest I know, larger in scale than the Villa Imperiale, with an orchestra pit and a set in sharp perspective flanked by gilded statues glinting in the sunlight culminating in a temple in the distance. The result is almost embarrassingly over the top. The driving force behind this particular garden was the first Hanoverian king's mother, the Electress Sophia, daughter of the Winter Queen, Elizabeth, and granddaughter of James I. Few British people visit the great German gardens but this is not one to miss on any account.

Why, you may ask at this point, this obsession with *teatri di verzura*? Well, no one who encounters one quite forgets the experience, for they have a significance far beyond being historical curiosities, evidence of the garden's role as a performance space. They are sharp reminders of a fundamental of good garden design which can be grasped at a glance in any of these theatres. And that is that a garden is about the manipulation of sight. Any garden, however small, is an arrangement of artefacts and plants calculated to draw the eye in a particular way; and the chief means of achieving that is still, as these green theatres show, perspective. And that's what makes them so relevant to gardeners even today: the lesson is there, stated in its crudest form, that converging lines and diminishing height give the illusion of distance. All that has to be done is to replace the proscenium in the mind's eye with the average downstairs back window overlooking the garden and the point is made. Everything we see depends on framing, how to arrange what we have within that frame to create vista, false distance and romantic illusion. The garden, in short, is your stage.

Garden visiting is hugely popular both at home or abroad, but how few people ever visit a garden and analyse even the most elementary of its effects. They just stroll through it, marvel, and rather take it for granted. With a little time and thought there is so much to learn as to how the great *coups d'oeil* of the past were achieved and how they continue to have lessons for handling even the smallest of spaces. A green theatre gives one this rudimentary jolt of recognising that it sets out to deceive, but you'll be surprised to discover how much in any well-designed garden in fact exploits exactly the same principles, although the proscenium may take the form of a pair of fastigiate evergreens, a pair of statues or urns or anything which frames and directs the eye. Take what you have learnt home and think about your own garden as a stage set, in which you and your guests are the actors and everything that you plant and build is your permanent – if seasonally mutating – set. It's not a bad way of beginning to master the principles of good design.

TROMPE L'OEIL

The expression *trompe l'oeil* is often thrown around in relation to garden design without, it seems to me, much thought as to what is really meant by it. Indeed, I'm not really sure that the use of the expression in relation to laying out a garden is that helpful. Most of us think of *trompe l'oeil* as something which essentially relates to painting. The baroque ceiling of a church is the most obvious example, where it seems as though the roof of the building has been taken off and we can gaze up into a sky in which angels and saints swirl around to infinity. But however does one cross from this to *trompe l'oeil* in a garden? That can be done only by analysing how that false illusion was achieved on the ceiling. The artist had in his armoury an orchestration of colour, light and shade, used according to the rules of perspective. Foreshortening gives us the illusion that the space and the figures extend upward when in reality they are perfectly flat areas of paint.

With that in mind I believe we can make the crossing into garden design. Everyone who makes a garden is doing something identical but in three dimensions instead of two, manipulating colour, light and shade through an arrangement of hard and soft surfaces to make a picture. Some of those pictures, however, can be more deceptive than others. It is in that latter category that I would firmly place *trompe l'oeil* in the garden.

Just to narrow the subject still further into manageable practical proportions I would divide these deceits of the eye into three categories. The most obvious and blatant one is that which uses precisely the trickery of the baroque ceiling we started with: the use of illusionistic scene painting as a witty form of garden ornament. That dissolves into a long tradition of three-dimensional figures in the garden placed to deceive, of which the multicoloured garden gnome is one of the more unfortunate instances. In the next group I would lump together deceits which are disguise, where something in the garden is pretending to be what it patently is not. A waterfall would be a good example of this, where we are led to believe that it cascades down from a natural stream beyond the bounds of the landscape but in reality it is the same water cycled round and round by a pump. The third category is a highly sophisticated one, for it is when the entire garden composition is arranged to make the visitor believe that this or that is larger or more distant than it really is.

These three categories at least give us something to cling to in a subject which quickly can drift off into the realms of the nebulous. Previous writers on garden design rarely essay the topic and I now know why. Going through my own library I could only discover one index which listed perspective at all and that was in Sylvia Crowe's *Garden Design* (1958) under 'perspective, false'. She writes:

> Many devices have been used in the past to increase the apparent size of gardens, from the painted *trompe l'oeil*, which suggests a non-existent view or extension of the garden, to the false perspective which increases the appearance of length in an avenue by narrowing the end ...
>
> The false perspective is of little value where the view may be looked at in reverse. But losing the boundary in shadow, or making it recede into the surrounding landscape, were devices of the English landscape school while the trees planted as stage wings framing the house at Stowe add both distance and emphasis to the view.
>
> Both these principles are among those which can be used in the small gardens of today ...

Unfortunately she doesn't develop the topic much, but at least we have a useful point of departure.

Let me begin by saying that I have never seen a successful painted *trompe l'oeil* in a garden. In the great gardens of the past a huge avenue could be terminated by an equally huge painted cloth. In the middle of the eighteenth century, London's Vauxhall Gardens were awash with theatrical *trompes l'oeil*. One walk ended in 'a beautiful landscape painting of ruins and running water' and another was terminated with a gothic obelisk which was, in reality, 'only a number of boards fastened together, and . . . covered with canvas painted . . .' As most of these were seen only by artificial light perhaps they worked, but I really cannot believe that they would deceive the modern eye. The sophistication of contemporary visual perception is such that painted vistas have no place in the garden of today. Nor do I think does deception by mirror glass, for I have never seen any that hadn't become smeared (although mirrors can be used to striking effect in spaces which are not alfresco, such as in a grotto or conservatory). One form of *trompe l'oeil* can, however, be marvellously successful; indeed it is a form of high garden wit whose essence is that everyone who sees it knows that the object is phoney anyway. The late Lady Juliet Duff awoke one birthday morning to look out of her window and find a celebratory obelisk in her garden. It was just like the gothic one at Vauxhall, a cut-out piece of illusionistic scene painting propped up from behind. I recall the life-size romantic eighteenth-century rider in E.V. Gatacre's garden at De Wiersse in Holland. Every summer this is brought out and sited in a different place in the surrounding woodland, providing a delectable *frisson* of times past.

These cut-outs call for the abilities of a theatrical scene-painter. They must be weatherproof and would need to over-winter indoors. An alternative is to buy silhouettes of features like standard trees in tubs which can be placed around the garden as witty eye-catchers.

Three-dimensional *trompe l'oeil* again used to be part of the garden's repertory of ornament, for the lead shepherds and shepherdesses of the Georgian age were once brilliant polychrome and sited to deceive. Woburn Abbey,

Bedfordshire, for instance, had a famous coloured figure of a woman weeder, but it would be a bold gardener who embarked on such a feature today. I've seen amusing stylised sheep dotted into a landscape garden, but if you are anxious to explore this aspect of garden deception visit the Grizedale Forest Sculpture Park near Windermere, Cumbria, in which you are likely to encounter, for example, a wild boar made of entwined brushwood. Such pieces open up intriguing possibilities for illusion in the garden in which the role of sculpture can be paramount.

Placing is, of course, everything, for such things work successfully only from afar. Close encounter shatters any illusion and the more dramatic it is the greater the necessity to keep the viewer at a distance. And this brings me to manipulation of perspective. In its gentlest form it can be used to make any little space seem greater than it is. Its most elemental form is the garden vista, where through a massing of trees and shrubs the eye is led into the distance. The massing either side becomes progressively closer until it is lost in the shadows suggesting more, or it frames what is called 'borrowed landscape', a view beyond the boundaries of one's own patch. Such an arrangement can, of course, be accentuated by colour, keeping the brightest in the palette in the foreground, reserving the softer hues for the distance.

For those with a garden leading directly on to countryside the ha-ha is the ultimate illusion, for the eye runs the two together oblivious of the rampart and ditch which separates them. But what about those with no landscape beyond to borrow? Oddly enough a garden gate which, in fact, leads nowhere can be a highly successful means of purveying an illusion of mystery and more beyond. The garden-writer

Mirabel Osler has used this brilliantly in the garden she has made in Ludlow, Shropshire. One cannot disguise the fact that here we cross into the sister art of theatre. And that means creating tableaux akin to those on stage, ones which really depend on the garden visitor wondering from afar. One effect is to plant an avenue of small trees gradually narrowing the path, or to do the same with a hedge. If the height of the hedge is also slightly diminished towards the furthest point, that will increase the depth. Best of all are the effects to be had if the land slightly rises. Placing an ornament at the end of such a vista makes it look monumental. In my own garden there is a six-foot obelisk at the close of a narrow walk on a gradient. It looks twice the height, but only as long as no one stands next to it!

I have not mentioned treillage, which has a long and honourable tradition as part of the armoury of garden deception. The simplest of all effects is still available even in ready-made ranges of trellis, in which the slats are made to suggest a receding tunnel or long window embrasure. One successful treatment is to train pyracantha or thuja into an outer containing arch.

A final word on disguise. The garden designers of the past never hesitated to build a ruin or place an eye-catcher on the horizon which was only a façade. A gardener's house seen from afar might be a druid's shrine. So why not hide the oil tank in a Greek temple or turn the toolshed into a hermitage? All it calls for is confidence and nerve and a sense of fun. There's not enough humour in garden design today. Rediscovering the tricks of false perspective, *trompe l'oeil* and disguise can lift the most prosaic of gardens into the realms of total enchantment.

RIVER GODS

I've still room for a river god in my garden. He would, of course, have to be god of the River Wye, which picturesquely wends its way about a mile from us at the bottom of the hill, running through Hereford and on to Ross-on-Wye. My wife's seventieth birthday is still a way off yet, so maybe I'll get that river god in time for the promised rill. There he'd recline, a venerable, hoary gentleman looped in draperies, his nude torso upright and one arm embracing the urn from which the water would pour. As the Elizabethans would have said, ''tis a pretty conceit'.

But like most conceits, the river god has its roots in historical truth. It is what we might designate an icon. There are river gods still spouting away like blazes from Caserta to St Petersburg, and all because of a stroke of genius by one man – the Italian architect Bramante who was commissioned to create a courtyard garden for Pope Julius II in which to house his collection of classical antiquities. The resulting statue court was once part of the celebrated gardens of the Villa Belvedere above the Vatican, on which work began in 1506. For the first time, a collection of antiquities was not only placed in a garden, but integrated into it architecturally.

Twenty years on, the Venetian ambassador identified our icon amongst the statuary in the Villa Belvedere garden: 'In the centre of the garden are two enormous men of marble, very ancient statues, and two fountains issue from them.' By this time there were two of them; the Tiber was the earliest, a figure who is said to have guided the Trojan Aeneas to found Rome. Soon after, at some point during his reign (1513–21), Pope Leo X had added a second, the Nile, and

Pope Clement VII (1523–34) was to add the Tigris, in a setting designed by Michelangelo. The Nile river god is still there but in what is now an unattractive eighteenth-century gallery of classical antiquities. The Tiber is now in the Louvre, having been carted off by Napoleon.

Not every garden owner in Renaissance Italy was rich or fortunate enough to acquire an antique river god, so it would have been but a short step to commissioning one, which is what both the Cardinals Farnese and Gambara did for their famous gardens at Caprarola and the Villa Lante at Bagnaia. There the river gods took on a new life, as elegant parts of each garden's sculptural composition, acting as symbols of the local rivers and streams rather than of the great rivers of myth and history. At Caprarola, the figures exude a muscular energy, supporting cornucopia which once spurted water into a vast urn. In contrast, at the Villa Lante, river gods are positioned reclining back to back, heavy and venerable. Both signal the arrival of the river god as part of the Italian Renaissance garden.

By the early seventeenth century, our icon is invading northern Europe. When Henri IV laid out Fontainebleau at the very opening of the century, the Florentine Francini brothers made the focal point of their huge canal garden the famous Fontaine du Tibre. Across the Channel, James I's queen, Anne of Denmark, was to have in her garden at Greenwich Palace another such figure. This time the statue was female, and designed by the great hydraulic engineer, Salomon de Caus. De Caus had seen the gardens of Italy, and went on to design an island in the shape of a river god for Anne of Denmark's eldest son, Prince Henry. When Henry died, his sister Elizabeth commissioned de Caus to design the legendary Hortus Palatinus in Heidelberg. His Rhine figure has now been rebuilt, and its waters now plash close to what remains of the famous grotto.

By the second half of the seventeenth century, river gods had become a baroque garden cliché and, in an age of absolute monarchs, a means of showing that even a country's rivers were subject to the king. What else could be their role in the *parterre d'eau* at Versailles? There an element of sexism enters, for the rivers are men and their tributaries women. But the quality of the bronze sculptures at Versailles can only be described as superb. Those, like me, who are devotees of Het Loo will recognize in the figures of the Rhine and Ijsselz there, back to back, a reworking of Caprarola and Bagnaia – but what of it? They preside from the terrace and give unity to its waters.

River gods had a potent life as long as a garden was meant to be read. The landscape movement hit our icon badly but, by the 1780s, Mrs Coade, the manufacturer of Coade stone ornaments, must have had a market – the river god she produced by John Bacon was, at £109, the most expensive item in her catalogue. One of her two survivors was once part of my empire at Ham House, when I was Director of the Victoria & Albert Museum. Marooned well away from water, he was designed to be a source for it. Would that one could buy a reproduction! It would solve many a problem.

If you are hunting for your own river god, do not despair if they seem elusive – around the Italian town of Vicenza, those workshops that are so adept at producing neo-baroque statuary will certainly run one up for you. One such figure nestles in the villa of Gianni Versace, fern bedecked, moss encrusted and exuding a trickle of water into the bowl beneath. I wonder what Bramante would have made of it all?

TOPIARY

From the time when I first started to plant my garden in 1974, I always intended that topiary should be part of it. The initial impulse was admittedly historicist, as I used to love going for walks in that wonderful series of engravings of English late seventeenth-century gardens in Kip's *Nouveau Théâtre de la Grande Bretagne*. These views remind us how very recent is our equation of gardening with the laborious maintenance of vast numbers of plant varieties. Until 'Capability' Brown and his followers destroyed those glories, whole gardens could be made up of nothing but grass cut into decorative shapes, trees planted in patterns, hedges, clipped evergreens and statuary. We need to rediscover the essential simplicity of those gardens whose pleasure arose entirely from their harmonious geometry as they responded to the qualities of lights of the successive seasons. Contrary to what we're told, those gardens were monuments to low maintenance, requiring nothing more beyond mowing in season and an annual clip made easier by today's mechanical shears.

Although there are now several books on topiary, they do not tell us much about how to deploy topiary in the design of the average small garden. On the whole, my advice is to use it sparingly, like statuary. And here I confine my comments to topiary proper as against hedges. Whether architectural or figurative, topiary is a strong statement. In a small garden one piece can form a focal point or four articulate a formal quartered space.

Even if you choose fast-growing plants, there must be a degree of patience in achieving your plan. It will take ten years to get a beautiful two-and-a-half-metre/eight-foot yew pyramid, but the intention will be there in five and the end result will be the envy of everyone and give your garden a sense of great style even on the dullest of winter days. Box, yew and holly have the great advantage of longevity and low maintenance, requiring only one clip a year.

There is a lot to be said for balancing these long-term projects with others of faster growth. The common hawthorn (*Crataegus monogyna*) makes a splendid quick standard, giving height to a formal garden, but you will need to clip it at least twice in a season. Golden privet (*Ligustrum ovalifolium* 'Aureum'), over-planted in pre-war suburbia, used with discretion can make fine focal points if clipped into strong shapes – cones, pyramids or standards. Even varieties of the dreaded Leyland cypress (× *Cupressus leylandii*) can be sculpted to effect.

Topiary doesn't have to be an esoteric labour. If you have a sure eye all those wire frames for training are unnecessary. I made my birds by clipping and pruning and tying the branches to get them to grow into shape.

A word of warning: I forgot to remove a wire tie. The almost-complete peacock turned russet brown and died. I was desolated to have to axe four or five year's work and wait for another shoot to create a successor.

Half the battle with topiary is waiting. But for those with a very large cheque book, few forms of gardening can be more immediate. Although I have not seen ready-trained yew, I have seen plenty of box standards, cones and spirals. There is quite an invasion of kitsch topiary in *Lonicera nitida*, which should be avoided.

And remember, you can achieve a topiary garden in containers. A series of box cones or standards in tubs can be arranged and re-arranged at will, even on the balcony of a flat or a roof garden.

It takes vision to embark on topiary. Ignore all so-called friends who tell you that you won't live to see it. To create a topiary garden which looks as though it has been there since Miss Jekyll's day takes precisely fifteen years. I know because I've done it.

ORNAMENT

We live in an age of the rediscovery of garden ornament. Ever since the last century, the golden era of the plant hunters, we have been plant obsessed, and only now are we beginning to look over our shoulders at the styles which preceded that explosion. Gardening depended for centuries on a very restricted range of plants but it accorded an equal status to other elements: water and the use of hard surface artefacts in the form of building or statuary. Indeed, some of the most spectacular early gardens consisted of little more than a perfectly proportioned and balanced combination of stone, water and clipped evergreens giving year-long satisfaction. Today we are discovering that such forms of gardening offer two advantages which are deeply attractive. As well as being low maintenance, apart from waiting for hedges and trees to mature, they are virtually instant.

The majority of us have small gardens, usually rectangular or L-shaped, and what we need to learn is how to adapt that style to such spaces, one central ingredient of which is ornament. The most important factors conditioning the choice of ornament are scale and site. The greatest mistake in terms of scale is the belief that a small garden calls for small ornaments. This is simply not true and nothing is more unhappy than a garden dotted with small-scale items like a china shop. A small garden calls, in general, for one stunning focal point and not a plethora of distracting incidental features. If your composition is formal it will naturally be sited in the centre or at the far end. If informal it will call for careful positioning to achieve asymmetrical harmony in relation to the planting. In a small garden that ornament will be the most important element in your garden's design. Unlike leaves and flowers it will be there at all times of the year and in all weathers and effects of light. Regard it as a major investment, like a good piece of furniture, and remember that the older and more weathered it gets the more valuable it becomes. Bear in mind too that, in an age of moving house, you can take it with you, provided you see that the lawyer excludes the garden ornaments from the sale contract.

Planning ornament in a small garden may be adding an extra element to an existing layout, or starting from an empty site. Whichever it is, make a plan on graph paper. In the case of an old garden, mark all the features in the way of trees, shrubs, paths and buildings. Ornament is a strong and exciting statement to make and you should never approach it as a mere afterthought. Carefully consider its position, for without doubt it will draw the eye and you will probably need to adjust existing features by eliminating some or pruning others to set off the ornament as the culmination of your garden picture. In the case of starting from scratch you will have all the advantages of planning a complementary design and planting around the artefact.

In designing a small garden you should start with that artefact and its positioning. You will certainly wish to place it in terms of vista as the crucial eye-catcher to the garden's composition. You will also almost certainly wish to glimpse it from at least one window in the house not only in summer but also in winter. Statuary capped with snow or under a crisp cold wintry sun has its own peculiar beauty of texture, light and shade. Always at least place a cane of the right height where you intend to site the ornament or even cut out a shape, however approximate, in card or plywood and stand it there to get the visual feel from every angle.

No major ornament should be less than four feet in height and it could be as much as seven or eight. Fountains, sundials, urns and obelisks would all make ideal free-standing focal points. So would large containers, remembering always that these mean a commitment to seasonal plantings at least twice a year. If the focal point is to find its home against a wall, a hedge or treillage, use busts on plinths or figurative statues which inevitably have uninteresting backs.

The architecture of your house must also be taken into consideration when choosing ornament. If it has classical features the whole repertory of the classical past is open to you. If it is modern your choice is far more restricted. I would suggest any of the obelisks, pure geometric form, or an urn.

And what of the background planting? Nothing sets off reconstituted stone features to greater effect than evergreens. A hedge or a niche of dense dark green yew is well worth the ten-year investment to get it to a height of eight feet. Thuja or × *Cupressus leylandii* will give you something of the same effect much faster but it will always fall short. A shrubbery with a heavy component of evergreens is also an ideal foil, having the advantage of shutting out unsightly views beyond and ensuring privacy. Depending on your soil, make it up out of shrubs such as *Prunus lusitanica*, *Viburnum tinus*, osmanthus, the mahonias, euonymus, *Fatsia japonica*, eleagnus and the camellias. In a small town garden an architectural framework of painted trelliswork can make an extremely effective setting for ornament, allowing for the use of a whole range of climbers from roses to the chaenomeles, from clematis to the honeysuckles. Free-standing ornaments can offer lovely planting opportunities too. If placed in a flower bed, an ornament can arise from a series of seasonal plantings held in by a permanent low hedge of green box, billowing lilac catmint or shrubby lavender.

If your garden is slightly larger a pair of ornaments might be a possibility, as pairs generally presuppose framing something beyond. A long narrow rectangular garden could be divided in two by a hedge with an arch or opening in the middle which would look splendid flanked by boy warriors, satyrs or rampant lions. Pairs would equally be handsome either side of a stone bench. Within a small garden there should be at least one seat. A bench is not an assertive object and, indeed, if important enough could be your focal ornament. New containers could be. I would counsel caution in their use in a small area, as the result can quickly be spotty. I would also favour sticking to ones of the same style, a pair or four, sited in such a way as never to detract or distract from the main eye-catcher. Close to the house, for instance, a pair of vases on pedestals can give great joy early in the year with a spring planting of bulbs to be followed by a summer one of geraniums or fuchsias and a winter sprinkling of pansies to give colour on even the darkest day.

Reconstituted garden ornaments are raw in colour on arrival and need the hand of time but that comes quickly, enabling them to mellow into the picture as moss and lichen form. But, as in all things, there are short cuts. The application of liquid manure, if you live in the country, is one way of attracting algae. Far easier, however, is yoghurt or sour milk. A cat is a sure source of the latter. Just tip the left-over milk into a container and pour or paint it over the ornament.

Ornament is part of the joy of gardening. It should, as with the furnishings of your house, be an expression of your personality. Do not hurry over choosing it, but make sure that when you do it will add that extra touch of distinction and delight both for you and for everyone who visits your garden.

GARDEN ARCHES

What is a garden arch? That, it would seem to me, is a useful place to start, for arches multiplied behind each other become tunnel arbours or pergolas and arches strung out in a line become arcades, although, just to confuse the issue, these can have arches set within them. Equally an arch frames and supports a gate, which again is separate garden feature. For present purposes these other features are excluded. Or rather, to misquote Gertrude Stein, an arch is an arch is an arch. In terms of materials it can be of wood, metal or even, in our own era, plastic. Exceptionally it may be of stone. And, of course, it can be grand, in heroic triumph or celebration, or equally humble, like a few larch poles cobbled together by a cottager to support a rampant honeysuckle.

The latter gives the arch its familiar role as a plant support, but in fact that doesn't feature much in its history before the last century. The prime function of the garden arch has been an optical one, to act as a frame to focus the eye, drawing both it and the feet onwards towards something, be it path, object or a magical glimpse into the beyond. And that means that there is a fundamental relationship between the arch in the garden and development and application of what we know as Renaissance optics to design. Now that doesn't mean that garden arches didn't exist in the Middle Ages, but they weren't used in that way. The only detailed picture we have of a royal herber, in a French manuscript of about 1465, has a delectable gothic garden arch that I would be happy to accommodate. But its purpose is admittance and it certainly is not designed to frame anything.

That change comes with the Renaissance and the establishment of new optical rules under the aegis of the architects Brunelleschi and Alberti, who invented, if that word is applicable, single-point perspective. In that way of perceiving the world converging lines and objects diminishing in size became the means whereby distance was expressed. This was a revolution which gradually replaced the old medieval polycentric way of looking at things and established as the norm the picture frame encompassing what was in essence a window looking on to a scene governed by those mathematical principles. The garden arch is in fact the picture frame in the garden. We only have to move on to the close of the sixteenth century to see how that changed and multiplied its use. Vredemann de Vries's *Hortorum Formae*, whose first edition appeared in 1583, provides us with a gallery of gardens, still in essence medieval but in which the medieval elements have been reordered in accordance with the new optics and the new classicism. De Vries invented the bird's-eye view of a garden, so it is hardly surprising that here we find the garden arch used relentlessly in terms of accentuating perspective vistas. Some of his arches are hugely elaborate, wooden architecture replete with columns, entablature and pediment. Others are quite modest constructions, but never wholly devoid of a little fashionable antique detail like a term. Nor should we forget that he includes a different kind of garden arch, the living one of clipped evergreens.

Carpenters' work was one of the great triumphs of Netherlandish gardening in the sixteenth century. It was a vehicle for affordable if transient grandeur and it was going strong all through the following century, as the delightful, if crude, woodcuts in *Den Nederlandtsen Hovenier* bear testimony. There's an entrancing naïveté about these arches, which makes it hardly surprising that the Pyghtle wrought-iron works were reproducing them in the Edwardian period as part of their repertory of Arts and Crafts garden ornament. Not for them the reproduction of what I would regard as the apogee of the garden arch, the treillage in the gardens of the palaces and great châteaux of Louis XIV's France. There, under the aegis of André Le Nôtre, the arch reached a superb elegance, which stands unrivalled.

It is now thought that it was the great architect Charles Le Brun who first suggested to Le Nôtre using what was the Dutch art of carpenters' work for porticoes and cabinets in their first great masterpiece, Vaux le Vicomte. Although iron decoration was often added, in essence virtually all of these garden arches were of wood, oak in fact, stained and painted. Their sudden proliferation arose from the need to superimpose some kind of architectural articulation on to the bosquets and cabinets of the wilderness areas of these vast gardens. They gave immediate spectacle to impatient owners. Nothing, surely, can ever match the effortless sophistication of these designs, but one cannot help but admit that they are very grand and therefore out of tune with our more egalitarian age.

With the advent of the eighteenth-century landscape style most of that went to the wall until the renaissance of the garden arch, engendered by the picturesque, by the advent of the rose garden (which called for them as supports) and by the arrival of suburban garden style as typified by nineteenth-century garden writers: first J.C. Loudon and then, for the masses, by Shirley Hibberd. In the age of mass manufacture, the catalogues of Harrod's and the Army & Navy Stores are awash with inexpensive garden arches. There they all are in every size and shape you can think of, and at a price to suit every pocket, in wire, wrought-iron and rustic work. Pretty they may be, but they're an apology after the architectural triumphs of earlier centuries.

There's not much to add to the story. In an age of gardening for Everyman the arch hasn't moved on in terms of design. What we can buy today is largely recycled pastiche from the Victorian age or, a bit later, Arts and Crafts stuff as seen in the Pyghtle catalogue.

But I've struck out a bit myself. Our worst disaster in twenty-five years of gardening was when our gardener misunderstood something I'd said and I suddenly alighted upon him demolishing to three feet high a nine-foot hedge trained into pilasters which was the culmination of one of our grandest vistas. What to do? Well, open the cheque book and draw breath. The solution was a reconstituted stone arch twelve feet high, which looks stunning bearing in Latin a great truth, CONDITOR HORTI FELICITATIS AVCTOR, or 'They who plant a garden plant happiness'.

THE GARDEN SHED

Our garden shed arrived by dint of our first builders over twenty years ago. They left behind them a small but useful hut with a pitched roof, solitary window and ailing door. In spite of the fact that tools and machinery to maintain the garden have proliferated over the years, filling a second shed opposite, that old clapped-out hut still remains the garden's sentimental horticultural hub. Whenever I go out to the garden I make it my first port of call, unlocking and then swinging – or rather dragging – open its door to go in and pick up my trug, checking that it contains what I need:

gloves, hand trowel and fork, secateurs and a foam-rubber kneeling-mat cased in a Sainsbury's plastic bag.

Checking is perhaps the key word, for this indeed is what you need to do with everything housed within the garden shed. I look at my gloves rent with holes, the fingertips missing, and make a note to buy at least another two pairs. And while I'm at it, why don't I splash out and buy another pad on which to kneel to weed? Then there's the trowel and fork, both OK, but one with a handle an insipid green which means that I mislay it in the undergrowth with a grinding regularity. Why is it that tool manufacturers always produce these small garden tools in shades of tasteful green or natural wood guaranteed to make them invisible? A distinguished garden friend each winter paints the handles of her tools a violent colour so that they hit the eye at once.

Any serious gardener must set aside time to get into that shed through the winter months to put everything in it, and also in the working areas in proximity, into good order for the coming season. Check all the tools and their condition, for you can't garden with faulty ones, and who knows – you could ask for replacements as Christmas presents. Machinery from mowers to petrol-driven shears will require servicing and shears sharpening. Do it now. And don't forget the wheelbarrow, for its tyre is bound to have a puncture. Then there's the interminable sorting. Canes and other forms of plant support must be stacked according to size, plant labels should be cleaned and put into a container, flowerpots need to be piled, also graded to size. Supplies should be gone through, a seemingly unending list running through bone meal, hormone rooting-powder, rose fertiliser, dried blood, lawn fertiliser, wire, string, wall tacks, tree ties and, if you use them, weedkillers and sprays. There's never time when spring comes, and it's fatal to enter the growing season with the garden shed and stores in chaos.

Gardeners' sheds, if you can ever get into them, have a certain fascination. I recall the tool shed in the gardens at Heligan in Cornwall, which figured in a television series. It stood not far from the melon frames and was a treasure trove of Victorian gardening implements, collectors' items by now. But it was the faint smell of damp which lingered in the mind and the way the light etched the ancient tools into sculpture. And then there was what could hardly be designated a shed at Powys Castle. That was something to be seen for its good order. The whitewashed walls were dotted with hooks and each hook had its own implement, a silhouette of which was outlined in paint direct on to the wall's surface. If you have the space this is a wonderful idea to copy. But once again it was the atmosphere which lingered, the shafts of a golden August light falling through the windows evoking a painting by the Dutch artist Sanraedam of one of those barn-like Dutch churches.

And while you are about it do look at the shed's external appearance. If it is hidden away, that's well and good – it really doesn't matter what it looks like; but often in a small garden it obtrudes into the vision. There's every kind of means of lifting its external appearance. It can be transformed into a decorative garden building by the addition of some gingerbread woodwork and painting. Today's DIY emporiums are a goldmine of mouldings and ready-made excrescences to tack on. And painting need not only be workaday. I recall one garden shed where the door had been transformed by a delightful *trompe l'oeil* still life in which a pussycat figured, staring out at me and making me smile. At the very least the shed can be disguised by the addition of trellis, either on to it or as a screen, and climbers. And there the possibilities are endless, depending upon aspect and your preference in terms of flower and colour.

COLOUR OF A DIFFERENT KIND

Colour in the garden. Where, so many ask, is it from December until early March? Many gardeners just give up, batten down the hatches and curl up with a book, waiting for the first yellow or purple crocus to poke through and catch the eye. Books on the garden in winter admittedly draw our attention to what little there is, such as the silky grey catkins of *Garrya elliptica*, the shiny brown trunk of the paperbark maple *(Acer griseum)*, the dependable if hardly inspiring lacy white flowers of *Viburnum tinus*, not to mention the hellebores, their petals flushed with purples, whites and greens. But it doesn't add up to very much really.

You have to peer closely for definite colour in winter, bar any berries which might linger on branches, having escaped the predatory birds. And what colour there is cannot be described as anything other than subtle and underplayed. The books which deal with colour in the garden aren't much help either; indeed they leave me with a fair amount of exasperation. The reason for this is that they never touch upon any other element which goes to make up a garden besides plants. To get really vibrant colour into your garden in winter you must learn how to jettison plant tunnel vision and open your eyes to a whole new perception of your garden, one that gets pleasure from artefacts.

It was visits to Russia and to Czechoslovakia, both countries with horrendous winters, which first stirred my mind on other possibilities for colour in the garden. There the baroque palaces and houses are painted in shades of pink, ochre, terracotta and yellow, including the buildings and other structures within the garden. Add to those colours touches of gold and even a garden under snow becomes a magic domain, a kind of architectural fantasy land. I remember returning from such a trip, stepping out of the car and looking at the side of the house, painted a safe good-taste grey-white and exclaiming, 'God, that is boring.' And so bright yellow it went, with blue treillage appliquéd right across it. That façade faces east towards the kitchen garden and catches the evening sun. Even on the dreariest winter's day my spirits are lifted by this joyful splodge of colour welcoming me back to the house.

But that was only the start of it. Timorously we began to apply this treatment across the garden on to buildings, ornaments, trellis, even simple plant supports. Two colours, a cinnamon ochre yellow and a marine blue, inspired by a colour seen at Smolny in Russia, now run right through the garden. To take one instance, a column, its shaft encircled with a relief of vine leaves and lizards, which until then had been waiting for the fashionable overlay of moss and lichen, was dramatically transformed by the paint pot. The pedestal has been washed in cinnamon, the shaft has its ground in blue so that the relief stands out dramatically and the ball on the top has been gilded. It looks stunning all the year but on a crisp frost-spangled morning, when the sun makes the gold flash and glint, the garden becomes a place of dreams, which is exactly what it should be.

Now that is what I mean by colour in the garden in winter. There's nothing revolutionary about it. Those lead shepherds and shepherdesses which used to be dotted around Georgian gardens were originally painted polychrome to pass as real people at a distance. Disneyland, I can hear someone say, but why not? And just think what the pagoda at Kew must once have looked like bedizened with no less than eighty garishly coloured and gilded dragons with tinkling bells in their mouths! In this way the past emancipates us from the dull conventions of the present. You may not have a pagoda but you will have a house which is the focal point of your garden. Why paint it a dreary colour when the rainbow beckons?

There are endless opportunities around the smallest garden for introducing permanent colour if you are bold enough, so strike out in the coming months and to hell with good taste. Everything from the garden shed to a plant support, from a flowerpot to a garden arch, is up for grabs when it comes to a lick of paint. The unnecessary cult of natural materials, stemming from the Arts and Crafts movement at the turn of twentieth century, has castrated our imaginations, which should run riot in the garden. As you look through your window there must be something that catches your eye ready for a quick lick of colour. You'll never regret it.

FRUIT TREES IN THE FLOWER GARDEN

Shortly after the orchard was planted I added a yew hedge to hide it. Foolish and ignorant man! A few years later I found myself cutting the hedge into swags and curlicues to get the full enjoyment of the trees. I had learnt a simple truth: that fruit trees are beautiful as a part of any garden's picture.

Which brings me to one of my favourite local expeditions. Westbury Court, Gloucestershire, is a house long gone but the National Trust rescued the garden at the close of the 1960s and has magnificently restored it. Laid out in the last decade of the seventeenth century, it is in the so-called Dutch style of William and Mary, and the great spectacle is the tall red-brick summer house that stands at the head of a long narrow formal canal in which the building is reflected. This is one of those garden tableaux that I stare at and know that I'll never be able to afford.

But that's not the point of this particular exercise, nor the simply astonishing evergreen oak, the largest ever recorded apparently and which must have been planted in about 1600. They all add to the delight of the visit, but I'm here for the fruit trees. These are deployed in two ways. One group is planted in proximity to a clipped-box parterre. This includes morello cherries, quinces, medlars and mulberries. The other, not to be missed, is espaliered along the very long west wall. Here are apples, pears and plums, their branches neatly stretching out towards each other bearing their green and rosy fruit. A narrow bed beneath is filled with lavender, love-in-a-mist and common marigolds. This is a chance to see a rare collection of fruits from the period with names like the 'Calville Rouge d'Hiver' apple, the 'Catalonia' plum and the

'Beurré Brown' pear. One is looking at a sight which was the norm in small to middling gardens until fruit trees became totally ghettoised into the orchard. It is a lesson in the compatibility of fruit and flowers which we need to relearn.

There still seems to be a resistance to mingling fruit and flowers, and yet there shouldn't be. Three centuries ago their presence was taken for granted. That prudish Puritan traveller Celia Fiennes records time and again the presence of fruit trees in the gardens of the period. Of Newby in Yorkshire she writes: 'The Squares are full of dwarfe trees both fruites and green, set crosswayes which look very finely.' They were there for their utility in an age before the supermarket and the apotheosis of the 'Golden Delicious'. Naturally every house aimed to be self-sufficient in terms of fruit. We may not be able to achieve that any longer in the small gardens of our own era but no garden should be without trees planted not only for the fruit but also because they contribute to the overall visual effect.

Apples and pears, if not plums or cherries, are handsome structural trees in any garden. What else brings spring flowers and autumn fruit which you can actually eat? And, you will know what you are eating devoid of the worry of what has been sprayed on to the fruit. If you seek out interesting varieties you will be assisting in the preservation of a fruit heritage under threat. Each tree has its history. In addition, if you buy them ready trained or are prepared to undertake the operation yourself, there is no end to the garden effects which you can obtain. More and more trees are available from specialist nurserymen trained as cordon, fans and espaliers. If you are lucky you might even hit on one which will supply you with palmettes. So instead of engulfing every wall with climbers, introduce a few espaliers. After all, you might just as well prune a fruit tree as a rose or clematis.

Two other old forms of gardening kept this mingling of flowers and fruit going into our own century. One was the French *jardin de curé* and the other was the Scottish pleasance. Both brought the orchard, kitchen and flower garden together as a single experience, with the flower borders generally acting as a screen for beds of vegetables. But my plea is to explore the use of fruit trees in your main garden design. Vegetables are labour intensive but fruit is not. Their maintenance demand is minimal beyond feeding and annual pruning. And, thanks to modern grafting, you can get trees of every size and for virtually any situation, from free-standing in a lawn to inserted into the flower border to planted in containers. You must of course check with your nurseryman that you have enough of a group to ensure pollination but you need do no more. And the fruit for the first couple of years must be removed as it forms to accelerate the tree's growth. From then on you're away.

RAISED BEDS

The discovery of the year in the kitchen garden has been raised beds, or sledges, as my wife, who is in control of that domain, calls them, referring essentially to their appearance, which, to my eye, is more akin to a series of moored rafts, several of them within a single large bed. We came to what to us is a new system of cultivation through both bitter experience and accident. One part of the kitchen garden was always subject to flooding, so when a neighbour kindly offered us a pile of railway sleepers we grabbed them and constructed our earliest raised beds to achieve better drainage. The existing beds were in effect divided into a series of compartments, leaving spaces between, along which to walk and tend the crops. Then a pile of common breeze blocks came our way and were put to similar use again with satisfactory results – so much so that we are piecemeal making the whole kitchen garden one of raised beds.

That garden is about the size of a tennis court and made up of ten beds each twenty by ten feet, with grass paths between and a broad central path running beneath a pergola in the middle festooned with honeysuckle and roses. It is not, I repeat, a decorative potager, which I tend to regard as one of the more foolish of recent horticultural fashions. Much as I admire them, they really don't belong to the real world of cooking and the kitchen. We can't spend our lives thinking about the vegetables we plant in terms of colour and shape combinations! As the cook, what I look for are wonderful things to eat. We grow our vegetables organically to cover as much of the year as we can manage, knowing their flavour and freshness to be unbeatable and dreading having to fall back on the supermarket for produce cultivated with we know not what. However, to return to the raised beds. Now each of our overall large beds has been subdivided by a series of rectangular raised beds, some orientated north–south, others east–west. They vary in width from four to six feet but are all about twelve feet long, the length in fact of some of the stout timber we now use which is of the kind available at any suppliers, about a foot wide and an inch thick. The boards are held in place by large wooden pegs.

I am aware that The Laskett kitchen garden is large, but raised beds are relevant even to the smallest garden. You will be amazed, as we have been already, by the extraordinary increase in produce. They have also revolutionised the running of the kitchen garden, for each bed is cleaned, double-dug and manured only when needed for seeds and planting out. Otherwise it is abandoned and allowed to run riot, sometimes for as long as a year or two, and then reclaimed. These beds are so easy to work because they are narrow and the containing edging is such that you can sit on it and weed. Also you can grow quite small quantities of a particular vegetable planted in short rows. Now we are in our stride we understand why they are such a success. In the first case no bed lacks proper drainage; in the second, as the earth is never trodden upon it is never compacted and therefore is far better aerated, so the soil warms more quickly and seeds germinate earlier, providing they are watered.

If I had read Ethne Clarke's excellent *The Art of the Kitchen Garden* (1988) earlier, I would have discovered all this, for she makes an eloquent plea there for raised beds, pointing a finger back at history. Up until the landscape age in the eighteenth century, all beds were raised whether they were flower, vegetable or herb. There are hundreds of prints and paintings showing such beds in the old medieval and Renaissance gardens. It had never occurred to me that this was anything other than a design feature, related to a style that was formal and geometric. I now realise that it reflected a horticultural reality: the results are better. It is difficult to establish when precisely the boarded bed ceased to be the norm. It was certainly there in the Jacobean writer William

Lawson's *Countrie Housewifes Garden* (1617). I guess they must have fallen from favour with the advent of the large walled kitchen gardens of the Georgian period, which must have been constructed with proper drainage channels. The polymathic writer and politician William Cobbett discusses the problems of kitchen garden beds in his *The English Gardener* (1829). There he writes about the earth being four inches above the gravel path and of the need to prevent the soil from spilling over on to it. There is no mention of boards: 'You must resolve to have an efficient protection for the walk; and this, I venture to assert, is to be obtained by no other means than by the use of box.' In this way the kitchen garden was to enter its Victorian zenith.

No matter, for as far as we are concerned what we stumbled upon has the proof of history. In the flower garden I'll admit raised beds still retain a place, particularly for grey foliage plants, and also for easy gardening for the elderly or disabled. But this is an appeal to those who love their produce to rethink their kitchen gardens and rediscover that fundamental element of the modest gardens of the farmers and yeomen of Plantagenet and Tudor England, the raised bed.

TIMEPIECE

There are two sundials in our garden. I treasure greatly the one that came from Cecil Beaton's garden at Reddish House in Broadchalke, Wiltshire. I recall him making a little lavender garden with this as its focal point at the close of the 1960s. As usual with Cecil, it was a fudged-up garden prop, the pedestal middle-European rococo I fancy, but the sphere, which sits on top of what looks like discarded handbell, must have been run up by the local blacksmith. It stands in the middle of our Silver Jubilee Garden, a happy memory of the man, but a useless timepiece. The second, far inferior, is of reconstituted stone and has enjoyed a fate, which it shares with many garden ornaments which can't quite be placed, of being trundled around the garden until finally it has come to rest beneath a sunless dome of pleached nut trees capped by a rampant *Rosa* 'Wickwar'.

It is astonishing how long the sundial has held its place as a cliché of garden ornament. Most gardening magazines have advertisements for them. As I write, the two main purveyors of reconstituted stone artefacts offer between them almost twenty different ones, all repro and none remotely reflecting anything that has happened in terms of the sculpture and decorative arts in this century. They range from a simple baluster to bulbous pedestals garlanded with drapery or flowers, their design provenance usually an ancient manor house. Both types are there: one the flat-topped dial marked with the hours with a gnomon casting the time, the second the armillary sphere in which a thin rod, usually shaped like an arrow, lies parallel to the earth's axis and serves as the gnomon. There's a fondness for inscriptions which reminds me of Mrs Alfred Gatty's splendid *The Book of Sundials* (1880), which lists over seven hundred mind-improving verses, mottoes and reflections. As I look at my digital watch, I have sympathy with the one on a sundial at Ladew Gardens in Maryland: 'I am a sundial, and

I make a botch, of what is done far better by a watch.'

The sundial is one of garden-making's harmless icons, providing a year-round vertical accent to hold together many a pleasing horticultural composition – or, at least, that is what it has become in our century. The early dials of Tudor and Stuart England were working objects, evidence of advances in the sciences of mathematics and astronomy. They were placed in gardens certainly but for function not for decoration. 'Sundials', wrote Reginald Blomfield, apostle of revived formality, in 1892, 'held an honoured place in the formal garden, sometimes on the terrace, sometimes in the centre of some little garden of lilies and sweet flowers.' Not quite true really, but by 1900 garden ornament manufacturers responding to this discovery were in overdrive producing the specimens we see around us in gardens today. The sundial appears almost as a signature of what was a new late Victorian garden style, the 'old-fashioned' or 'old-world' garden.

That movement was typical of the 1880s and 1890s, a kind of gardening off-shoot of the Pre-Raphaelites and the revived Queen Anne style. It favoured clipped yew rooms and topiary, and the use of old herbaceous plants and climbers. We are on a line of descent which leads us down to Arts and Crafts-style gardens and that *locus classicus*, Hidcote. The sundial runs alongside it and we see them sprout up everywhere in photographs and watercolours of gardens before 1914. By then the sundial, along with the style, had migrated to suburbia, for its relatively unintimidating scale allowed it to be adapted into extremely modest spaces. No wonder that even today the average garden centre has a neat row of them ready for purchase.

But wouldn't it be marvellous if some of those manufacturers of ornaments could move on? Surely someone must be capable of designing a sundial which would be of our own age and not a nostalgia trip? I've seen a handsome one by Henry Moore but those that most stick in my mind are by Sir Mark Lennox-Boyd, both in his own garden (he is married to the garden designer Arabella Lennox-Boyd) and at Holker Hall in Cumbria. These sundials are quite extraordinarily complex objects telling of the movement of the heavens in such a way that Isaac Newton, who designed a dial for himself, would have approved. They rediscover the real purpose of such things and don't reduce them to being garden props. They remind us that scientific advance and gardens at one time went hand in hand with the garden as a laboratory. So what I am really trying to say is that in the new century wouldn't it be exciting if the garden sundial were rethought and became an emblem not of past times but of those to come?

Author of books on popular gardening

Mrs Earle
Maria Theresa EARLE
1836-1925

HERBALIST

IOANNIS GERARD

1545-1612

GARDENERS & GARDENING

I have been lucky enough to have known some of the most distinguished practitioners of the art of gardening this century, the majority of whom, I'm glad to say, are still with us, although a number have passed on. One who crossed my path early on was Russell Page but I was so ignorant then that I hadn't keyed into the fact that I was talking to one of the great gardening figures of the age. I remember him as a large taciturn man, casually dressed and with a huge satchel over his shoulder, stuffed with rolls of paper.

Geoffrey Jellicoe was another matter, a lovely teddy bear of a man, rotund and with a twinkling eye. We had to do a joint presentation on gardens before Queen Beatrix in the palace in Amsterdam. Poor Geoffrey: his aged feet needed the comfort of slippers in the royal presence, which worried him. But I told him firmly that she wouldn't notice and, of course, no one did. I saw him last at Sandringham where he came to talk to me about the garden he'd made there for George VI. He had never seen it since it was planted after the war, but I recall his main interest focused on the large gin and tonic which came at lunchtime. I've met few other people who exuded such affection and generosity of spirit. He remains an example to which to aspire.

Mien Ruys is still with us in her late nineties. Who she? I hear someone asking. Well, arguably this Dutch woman is the Gertrude Jekyll of the latter half of the twentieth century, the person who set garden style for the new age of democracy using railway sleepers, decking and plastic. She arrived to meet us in a wheelchair on a chill autumn day, an old tea-cosy of a hat down over her ears. Then she peered up and her intelligence radiated. 'I have been gardening for seventy years,' she said. 'Do you like my garden?' Indeed, I assured her, I did. Someone then reminded her that she had met Gertrude Jekyll. 'Yes, I am the last living person who spoke to her.' 'At Munstead?' I asked. 'Yes, at Munstead.' That was living history.

JOHN GERARD

The year 1997 was the quatercentenary of one of the most famous of all English garden books. The handsome engraved title page reads as follows: *The Herball or Generall Historie of Plantes Gathered by John Gerarde of London Maister in Chirurgerie. Imprinted at London by John Norton. (1597).* In this way one of the best-loved garden books in the English language made its debut almost a decade on from the defeat of the Spanish Armada. Gloriana was in her sunset years, her radiance undimmed, the living embodiment of the resurgent confidence which gave this country a golden literary renaissance as the century moved to its close. Across the river from where Gerard gardened in Holborn, London, Shakespeare's histories were on stage. The *Herball* still casts its spell on even the most casual of dippers because Gerard was writing in the first full flowering of the English language. This book seems to inaugurate a great tradition, one which is thankfully still with us today, of botanical and horticultural writing that can also belong to mainstream literature. We may not read Gerard for information any more, but we do for sheer pleasure.

Who can fail to be spellbound by even one sentence from

the dedication of this book alone? 'What greater delight is there than to behold the earth apparelled with plants as with a robe of embroidered worke, set with Orient pearles and garnished with rare and costly jewels?' To turn its pages is to revel in unalloyed delight. It is a mixture of pioneering botanical record intermingled with folklore and Gerard's own hands-on observations. His plant knowledge came from studying the Home Counties, Kent, Essex and Surrey; nor should we forget that his London was a network of gardens. Together this makes for an irresistible combination. 'Walking in the fields next to the Theatre by London,' he alights, for example, upon a double buttercup; 'upon the brick wall in Chancery Lane, belonging to the Earl of Southampton [Shakespeare's patron]', his eye falls upon a saxifrage; while of the 'Herb Two-pence' he writes, 'I found it upon the banke of the river Thames, right against the Queenes palace of White-hall.' All through, the book is touched by this humanity, which makes him take us as it were on a stroll through late Tudor England catching the colour and scent of its herbs and flowers.

His account of some of our earliest garden flowers is pure enchantment to read. 'There are at this day under the name of *Cariophyllus* comprehended divers and sundry sorts of plants . . . some whereof are called Carnations, others Clove Gillofloures, some Sops in Wine, some Pagiants, or Pagion color, Horse-flesh, blunket, purple, white, double and single Gillofloures . . . also those flowers we call Sweet-Johns and Sweet-Williams.' Of rosemary: 'If a garland thereof be put about the head, it comforteth the brain, the memorie, the inward senses and comforteth the heart and maketh it merry.'

Here speaks the superintendent for three decades of the

great Lord Burghley's gardens both in the Strand and at his palace of Theobalds in Hertfordshire. Then there is Gerard's own garden in Fetter Lane, Holborn, which boasted no less than a thousand species. These he published in 1596, in the earliest list of plants ever of a private English garden. Alas, we do not know what his garden looked like, but it must have been strictly geometrical with raised beds arranged in a formal pattern, the plants about three feet apart in a way we would find strange, for we have been spoilt with plant profusion. Each would have stood proud with space around it so that the visitor could wonder at each plant and be able to appreciate it from every angle, much as one can the woodcuts in the *Herball*. That indeed captures, too, in its pages all the excitement of the plant explosion of Renaissance Europe. A great lord like Edward, Lord Zouche, whose passion for plants is said to have cost him his patrimony, sent Gerard seeds from Crete, Spain and Italy. Plants came too from his friend Jean Robin, *arboriste et simpliciste* to the last Valois kings of France. And then there were the London merchants whose commerce took them across the known world: men like Nicholas Lete, who sent Gerard 'a Gillofloure with yellow flours' from Poland.

Poor Gerard was to be accused of plagiary, that his book took over someone else's translation of the Rembert Dodoens' *Pemptades*, but that great scholar of our botanical and horticultural literature Blanche Henrey stoutly defends him against the charge. All through the *Herball* we are reminded that every plant then had a double function, for Gerard was a surgeon and indeed ended up Master of the Barber–Surgeons Company in 1607 just five years before his death. He stares out at us from his engraved portrait, somewhat schoolmasterly in doublet and gown, one hand resting upon a book, the *Herball* one assumes, the other clutching a spray of potato foliage with flower and berry. 'I have received roots hereof from Virginia,' he recounts, 'which grow & prosper in my garden as in their native country.' In his dedication to Lord Burghley he records: 'To the large and singular furniture of this iland, I have added from forren places all varietie of herbes and flowers that I might in any way obtaine . . .' Well might we celebrate Gerard's *Herball*.

MOWING

I feel a bit like Gwendolen in *The Importance of Being Earnest* when it comes to mowing. To Cecily's withering, 'When I see a spade I call it a spade', Gwendolen retorts with the put-down: 'I am glad to say that I have never seen a spade. It is obvious that our social spheres have been widely different.' Well, I have seen a mower, several, but in my all twenty-three years of gardening I've never actually used one. In fact, three mowers cope with our acreage, two for the finer grass and one which looks like an oil tanker that we call the jungle-buster. That comes into its own each mid-August when the long grass is at last cut. The latter is in the main in the orchard and along each side of the pleached lime avenue where the main naturalistic plantings of spring bulbs are. Never cut earlier than this, to allow them to store energy for next year's flowering and for primroses and cowslips to self-seed. Years ago I recall asking Lady Salisbury how she achieved the miraculous carpeting of primroses at Cranborne and being told that the secret lay in this very late cutting.

But to return to the subject of mowing. This is one of gardening's really boring chores, going on seemingly for months. Its only virtue is that the person wielding the machine sees the results of his labours instantly, in the main a sheet of tranquil green, an essential foil to all that surrounds it in the way of flowerbeds and shrubberies. But, with a little thought, mowing could be so much more than that; indeed it has the potential of becoming a major contribution to any garden's design, for the correct orchestration of areas of short as against long grass can produce quite magical effects. Paths can be made, creating vistas or serpentine walkways; piazzas can be delineated accentuating, for instance, a central feature such as an ornament or tree. The possibilities are endless. Nor need the difference be only between the grass which is cropped and that which is left to grow long before mid-August felling: it can also be between grass of varying lengths. All that has to be done to achieve this is to adjust the level of the blades.

The first time I was struck by this effect was some years ago when I was involved in filming at the Dryden family's house, Canons Ashby, in Northamptonshire, which had just passed to the National Trust. On one side of the house the land fell away, sculpted in the seventeenth century to form a series of descending stately terraces. The one at the bottom had the grass cut at two different heights in order to create an exedra emphasising the garden's geometry. It made clear to me that modern mowing machines have the possibility within them of adding to the visual excitement of a garden in terms of ground-level pattern, of a kind which could either be year-round or just seasonal. Few garden designers, however, seem to give thought to this. Two other points. If a year-round scheme is opted for, when frost comes or snow falls it will delightfully emphasise the pattern you have cut on your grass, providing unusual winter interest. The second is that grass left longer is far more drought resistant than when it is close-cropped – something to bear in mind as we begin to make adjustments to garden style in response to global warming.

One artist-designer who is a sophisticated exponent of this art in public spaces is Graeme Moore. So much so that he is unafraid of flying that long-forgotten kite, the garden without flowers. He makes gardens simply by cutting grass at different levels. These he calls 'Herbe Gardens', borrowing the French for grass. He dispenses with flowerbeds and borders, ornaments, paths, walls and statuary, indeed all those elements which we now look on as essential to garden-making. Instead, he makes a deeply satisfying garden by articulating the grass into patterns of long and short areas forming circles and squares, axes and cross-axes, sometimes even mowing bold serpentine baroque rhythms. In this he echoes, in late twentieth-century terms, voices from the past, for until the plant explosion of the Victorian age, descriptions of some of the most admired gardens never even refer to flowers at all.

Now I am not counselling such an extreme approach to the average garden but there is a green thought or two here upon which to ponder. There's plenty of time through the summer to experiment with pattern mowing. It must relate, of course, to your machine and it is a prudent idea to draw a sketch on a piece of graph paper of your intentions. A hard surface path, for instance, which may lead to a lawn, could be made to continue in a straight or winding form across the greensward simply by letting the grass on either side grow longer. Maybe there's a vertical accent, a sundial or a statue, which can be emphasised by close mowing round it or indeed by doing the reverse. By working out a design schedule for mowing you will actually reduce the mowing load. I know, there's no way of ducking that terrible mid-August massacre when the long grass has to be not only cut but raked up by hand. But remember, that's only annual and you'll be more grateful next spring when your earliest flowers have multiplied and are more beautiful than ever. And if your first essays in pattern mowing are a disaster just let the grass grow and try again!

TRAINING YEW HEDGES

To misquote the popular song: 'Yew, wonderful yew, it had to be yew.' And who wouldn't, if you are among those who've had to suffer all the scorn of visitors who crow at length on seeing your newly planted hedge: 'You'll never live to see it.' Rubbish. Admittedly, it's not a hedge for those who move house every five years, but if you've put your roots down firmly, so to speak, plant it.

I write this because we're in the month when we cut our hedges, a task at The Laskett divided between our heroic gardener, Robin, and myself. But to start at the beginning.

We planted the cheapest and smallest yew, about two feet high, and you can reckon that with an annual feed it will grow about a foot a year. Don't ever cut the leader until it reaches the height which you require it but do trim the sides. The ideal hedge, the books say, should have a batter, that is the sides should gently slope and narrow to the summit. Ours don't because I didn't learn about that until later and really I quite like them boldly and exactly vertical. My main problem is that in places the foliage isn't thick to the ground. Lawrence Johnston obviously had the same problem at Hidcote, I once noticed, and infilled the gaps with box, which seemed to work perfectly well.

The first few years of growing a yew hedge are agony. You can count on a few losses but year eight is the dramatic turning point. By then the hedge should be about four to five feet high and the great thrill, if you are making a green room, is that for the first time you can sit down and not see out of it! I remember being bowled over with excitement by this, realising that I'd grown architecture and added mystery. By year fifteen, your hedge ought to look as though it was planted before 1914.

But to return to cutting. Do, I implore you, think about that from the moment the hedge goes in. Make drawings on a piece of graph paper, one of the elevation and a second of the ground plan. Get inspiration from books or looking at yew hedges in other people's gardens. Cut the bed for the hedge into the ground-plan shape. Articulate the hedge wall with ramparts, pilasters, towers or windows, and crown its summit with an interesting silhouette: crenellations or curlicues, spires or pompons. For cutting the top, keep to hand a copy of your scheme and, with judicious clipping each year, see the hedge fill out into the shape you have planned. In winter, in particular, when the light falls across it, you will be grateful for having conceived it in terms of a building's façade.

Lucky ones may have a yew hedge already. Spring is the time that you can start reshaping it. Again, draw up a scheme. In the case of the sides all it means is leaving this year's growth where you want a pilaster or bastion. When it comes to the top, wait until the autumn if you wish to cut down into it to form swags or crenellations. If you want to let it go upward again, let it sprout where you need it to. At the least, add a few cakestands or lollipops. In that case, just select the leaders and let them go up. They'll take two or three years but they'll soon be there. I've just done this with a young yew hedge only about three feet high. My intention is to emulate that wonderful hedge at Knightshayes in Devon where hounds chase a fox along the top of the hedge. In my case it's going to be prancing pussycats all round the little garden!

Here we use hand shears and petrol-driven cutters. I have avoided the electric ones ever since I severed a cable with a bang. It's amazing how much you can cut in an afternoon. All the twiddly bits are done by hand as works of art and love. On the whole we take care to keep hedges at an easy working height, that is reachable from one of my best garden buys, a set of rolling office steps with a platform balcony at the top and with a brake. It has transformed our annual cutting operation and copes with hedges up to ten feet high. Before that I used to balance on a pair of aluminium steps, one leg of which usually used to sink into a mole channel, keeling me over.

Although Vita Sackville West and Harold Nicolson fled

Sissinghurst for July and August, I regard these as also wonderful garden months. You can stand back and admire your handiwork, happy in having restored your garden's structure. What could be more rewarding? And with yew, you can do a good deed. Yew clippings are desperately needed in order to produce the new anti-cancer drug, Taxol. We have sent Yew Clippings Ltd over thirty large sackfuls, but smaller amounts are welcome. The clippings must be clean and fresh and also unadulterated by sticks, stones or leaves. Doing this has sharpened our yew clipping operation and I can't recommend it enough. The demand for successful yew-based drugs, I understand, is still increasing – every reason for planting that hedge this autumn.

ALL CHANGE

The grass has had its final cut. The leaves have fallen from the trees. The borders have been cut down and put to bed. The last sad bonfire of autumn has sent its smoke swirling up into the atmosphere. Now is the time for every gardener to draw back the camera's lens of his eye and take a long hard look. Few do. Most of us are so obsessed by close-focus detail and the tasks which have had to be done that we never take a fresh look at our garden's composition. If you have kept a photographic record (which I regard as essential) get it out and trace your garden's development – what you started with, how you altered it and, above all, how everything has burgeoned or not as the case may be. Just doing that not only gives one a sense of achievement but stimulates the critical faculties.

Visitors to our garden have often said something on which I ponder. 'The wonderful thing about both of you,' the comment ran, 'is that you're always altering things, always embarking on new projects.' 'Doesn't everyone?' I replied. 'No,' came the answer, 'the majority of people just lay their garden out and that's it.' How unutterably boring and unimaginative, I thought. Gardening, like life, is an adventure to be savoured to the full and winter is the season during which to renew the quest.

The reason for that is that we can see the garden's bones so very clearly: hard surfaces in the way of paths, steps, containers, walls, ornaments and buildings as well as evergreen shrubs, both those allowed to grow as they would wish and those which by clipping and pruning we torture into shape. Ask yourself, does it all work? Does the picture now in these chill months when stripped back still give pleasure? For it should. The measure of a good garden is winter and winter is the season for major alterations and amputations.

Last year, for instance, I was busy lower-limbing some thirty-foot-high conifers, cautiously working up the trunk branch by branch, taking care always to stand back to check on what was revealed until the vista to the flower borders that I was after was composed. Be cautious. Once a branch is severed, you can't put it back.

At the moment we're busy introducing paths across the orchard. One we discovered presented the opportunity for a fantastic new vista but it called for the bravery to cut through and reshape a perfectly clipped eight-foot-high yew hedge in the Rose Garden, which I'd waited twenty years for. Somehow I had to prise the hedge apart to stick my head into it to see whether it was worth the candle. It was, but my heart was in my mouth as we gingerly cut through. The new perspective is stunning, although I know that I'll have to wait five years before the old hedge grows into its new shape.

A word about skyline again. Scan it carefully and check that it is pierced by an interesting panorama of feathery branches and columnar evergreens. If there are gaps plant something now.

Remember, too, that fibrous-rooted plants – those that can be moved, taking care always to take with them plenty of earth. This is the time to re-site them to better advantage. These are also the months in which to thin out, for all of us overplant initially. But remember that there are other ways than chopping a tree or shrub down. There is always the possibility of reducing its size dramatically by shaping it with saw and secateurs into some form of topiary or pleaching. Ornaments, too, can be shifted around, for generally they do not find their most advantageous siting first time.

My main message is never to be timid, never to shrink from being decisive. If something is nearing the end of its life or is just plain ailing, bite the bullet, rip it up and throw it away. You'll be amazed by the sense of relief that such brutal action brings, for chopping something down releases a new vision and enthusiasm. All the time during these crucial and most exciting months of winter, you will be forming your garden picture for next year – but that will only be as good as the structure you put in place now.

COMPOST

One of the most touching gestures at the funeral of Diana, Princess of Wales, was her brother Lord Spencer's gathering of the bouquets of flowers banked at Althorp's gates and scattering them across the island on which his sister was buried. They will, he said, in due time contribute to producing more flowers. Compost of a sort, yes, but who could not fail to be moved by this touching tableau of the cycle of death into new life?

We came to the cult of compost late and that I now bill my wife Compost Queen of Herefordshire we owe to a visit to Princess Sturdza's astonishing garden just outside Dieppe. Every plant you have ever encountered, it seems, grows for her at least twice the size, and much can be attributed to her systematic application of organic compost. In six weeks beech leaves, laced with Quick Return Compost Action, somehow turn to a rich sooty compost. Such is her passion that this formidable lady is to be sighted each autumn combing the streets of Dieppe in search of yet more leaves.

This visit acted as a kind of Pauline conversion on my wife. Now visitors to The Laskett garden are suddenly stunned as they stroll from the ordered elegance of the orchard to the kitchen garden by an apparition akin to an exploded minefield made up of at least a dozen large mounds caged in with black plastic, held down by old rubber tyres, interspersed with the odd oil drum with a makeshift lid weighted down by a stone. It is by no means a beautiful sight but it has become the heart of the garden and has produced a veritable renaissance in everything that we grow.

We are lucky. We have space. The more space you have, the

more you can leave nature to take its course and we now reckon on a four-year cycle for the average heap. Leaf mould is, of course, kept separate for the turn-round is quick, as little as just a year, and it is reserved for plants like our hellebores, which just love it. The old oil drums contain our worm directly on the soil, but apply in thin layers to activate the other compost heacompost, the bottoms removed to allow the worms to penetrate. Into them goes a rich mix of kitchen waste, including things like the contents of the vacuum cleaner and fish offal which produces a steamy gunge very quickly. Cover it, or else it will be raided by predators. That gunge we don't use ps. All our newspapers are shredded and layered up between hot and sticky grass cuttings through the summer months with stinging nettles and the odd bunch of self-sown comfrey acting as a supercharge for heating up the heaps. When it comes to shredding, do purchase a heavy and not a lightweight shredder, and do follow the safety instructions.

Our second inspiration was a visit to the Henry Doubleday Soil Research Association organic garden at Ryton outside Coventry. I can't recommend this enough as an experience of hands-on no-nonsense gardening. Here, compost-making is preached with an almost evangelical fervour. What is more, they have on display every bin currently available on the commercial market. In a survey which they took four years ago, they recommended wood as the most appropriate material as it provides some insulation and 'breathes', so the compost is less likely to get wet. But few of the models they examined were in fact satisfactory. One cubic metre is usually recommended for fast, hot composting but in fact the majority of the bins are smaller than this, averaging out at between 200 and 300 litres.

As I see it, compost-making has been taken over by those who thrive on consumer marketing and who attempt to turn it into a genteel tidy pastime, in a neat little container which is in a corner of your garden and to which you point as a demonstration of your adherence to organic principles and your care for the environment. This is designer horticulture. I admit that when my wife started on her compost crusade I was transfixed by the ugliness of it all. A decade and more after, I've become an apostle for screening off a fair section of the garden as a workshop area. Making compost is messy and untidy and it stinks to high heaven and you'll get filthy doing it. Those starting gardening are so often misled by design books with 'inspirational pictures' but which sweep areas for practicalities under the carpet. Don't stint from the outset of planning to allocate as capacious an area as you can as an operating dump, screened of course. In the case of compost-making allow room for two containers, one for leaf mould and a second for worm compost, and allow at least one or more spaces for general compost. It's hard work, I know, but you'll never regret it. Oh, and compost has inspired some of the worst garden poems I know, which include lines like 'Of composts shall the Muse descend to sing . . .' and 'Behold this compost! behold it well! Perhaps every mite has once form'd part of a sick person – yet behold!' You have been warned.

MRS C.V. EARLE

The year 1997 marked the centenary of Queen Victoria's Diamond Jubilee, but it also marked the the centenary of the publication of an all-time Victorian garden bestseller, Mrs C.V. Earle's *Pot-pourri from a Surrey Garden*. This book was to go through no less than twenty-nine editions, almost twice as many as William Robinson's far more important *The English Flower Garden* which had appeared a decade and half before. So great was its success that it was to encourage its sixty-one-year-old author to write *More Pot-pourri* and, unbelievably, *A Third Pot-pourri*, besides a handful of other books including a personal memoir entitled *A Scented Life*. The National Trust, quite rightly in my view, republished the first book in 1984 amongst their series of classics, with an excellent introduction by Susan Campbell.

This book was enormously influential in spreading the style we associate with William Robinson, jettisoning High Victorian bedding-out for a return to native herbaceous plants disposed in a manner which we would recognise today. It not only spread the message through the British middle classes but was hugely influential in America. The format of the book is a very simple one: a series of semi-diary entries under the months, in which the author describes what is happening in her garden with tips on what to do and a recommendation of plants to grow. It is difficult to think that she could have hit upon this formula without the immediate precedent of another late Victorian classic, Canon Henry Ellacombe's *In a Gloucestershire Garden* which appeared in 1883 (and has also been reprinted by the National Trust). Ellacombe's book is far better written and far more professional than Mrs Earle's discursive ramblings. In her case within a couple of pages she can meander through cursing self-seeded Welsh poppies to astrantias and from thence to garden peas and how to cook them. Indeed, great chunks of the book are taken up by her listing the contents of her garden library and with recipes for what she describes as 'dainty dishes' of a kind we would regard today as inedible, everything swimming in a béchamel or brown sauce. And, feeling perhaps that what she offered was a bit short, she tacks on to the end a series of quite weird, disconnected chapters on daughters, sons, furnishing, amateur artists, health and a visit to London!

None the less, there is something oddly compulsive about this book. Much that she writes about, bound as it is into the cycle of the seasons, rings an eternal bell: 'On going into a garden one knows by instinct . . . if it is going to interest me or not', or 'Gardening is, I think, essentially the amusement of the middle-aged and old.' Maria Theresa Villers, as she started out life, was in fact a radical, proud of her descent from Oliver Cromwell, and a follower of Ruskin, William Morris and the Pre-Raphaelites. Looking at the formidable square-jawed matron in her photograph it is difficult to believe, but it was so. Like Gertrude Jekyll, she studied at the South Kensington School of Art and drifted at one time towards the fringes of Victorian Bohemia, which she rejected as having an 'undesirable atmosphere'.

What is interesting is what the book conceals as much as what it reveals. We can gather that she had a cook and a gardener but who and what else we never learn. We never really get the impression either that she was in fact rich, her husband inheriting a fortune. That reticence I think must partly explain the success of her book, for she writes as one of a horde of anonymous late Victorian women who were married, comfortably off and living in the suburbs of London while their husbands commuted into the city to work each day. Her house, Woodlands, at Cobham in Surrey, surrounded by two acres of garden, replicated that of thousands of others going up at the time. To those women she offered reassurance, taking them by the hand and introducing them to one of the occupations which they could do, apart from running the house: gardening. And along with it she made them followers of the new garden style. Here at Woodlands is the tennis court, the croquet lawn, the tiny rockery and goldfish pond, the rose beds and herbaceous borders we still see flourishing even today in the stockbroker belt.

But just why was the book so incredibly successful? A clue lies perhaps in another centenary celebrated in 1997, that of the magazine *Country Life*. That was founded with the aspiring classes of late Victorian England in mind, those who built Arts and Crafts houses in the commuter-belt radius of London. And the new magazine's chief garden writer was to be Gertrude Jekyll whose collaborator, the architect Edwin Lutyens, was to marry one of Mrs Earle's nieces. There's another clue also in a remark she makes about a book which had inspired her. 'It's a fascinating chat about a garden to read in a town and dream over . . .' Garden writers like myself have been kept in business thanks to this factor ever since.

HAIRCUT TIME

This is haircut time. No, not for me but for the vast mileage of yew, beech, box and × *Cupressocyparis leylandii* hedging which makes up the structural bones of The Laskett garden. We usually start with the box. There's a knot garden and two parterres, not to mention beds edged with it or the small forest of topiary accents, balls and cones dotted all over the place. Let's face it, I'm in love with box of any kind, grateful for its year-round permanence, the rich glossiness of its leaves and the fact that it can be clipped into almost anything.

Most of our box is the dwarf variety (*Buxus sempervirens* 'Suffructicosa'). It is, I'm afraid, subject to frost and the result of a late one is that gorgeous sprigs of new growth can be reduced overnight to fronds of a deadening pale beige. If I were starting again, I'd opt for *Buxus macrophylla*, which is also small leaved, but far tougher. The garden is full of all sorts of box because we've pulled bits off here and there over the years and grown them on. What we have ranges from gold-tipped to golden through to grey-blue besides quite a range of vigorously coarse-leaved varieties, but what they are I know not. The Rose Garden beds are edged with what I call 'Verey quick box' which came from Rosemary Verey's garden at Barnsley, in Gloucestershire and whose encouraging habit is betokened by its name.

The wonderful thing about parterres and knots is that they're there from the moment that you put in the plants. For the rich there's no problem because the cheque book can be opened and what is virtually a full-grown effect can be achieved at once. For the rest of us, it's small bushy plants, usually about six inches tall, planted about the same distance apart. When starting on such a project it's quite good to splash out and buy a few fully grown topiary specimens to act as anchors to any composition. But I'm amazed by how many people, having done the initial planting, are seized with a kind of horticultural panic when it comes to the first year's cut. I am perpetually being asked about cutting, the mechanics of it, when and how and how often. So here's my box routine. When to cut? The answer is any time. Remember that young box is far more vigorous than old. The earliest attempt at a box parterre here is now twenty years old and occasionally it grows so little that I can skip a year. In contrast the young box generally calls for two trims a season and I'd opt for late June for the first when other elements in the garden are getting decidedly frothy. It's good to see the sharp contrast of the architecture restored. And, if it grows a lot, I do it again in September.

The first year is always the great test, for there is an understandable reluctance to cut down dramatically a plant which seems so slow to grow. It is essential that you do so, removing virtually all the vertical growth, leaving that at the sides to bush out. If you don't, you'll end up, as I have done several times, with leggy plants. That problem can be solved either by digging up and planting the box deeper or by infilling and raising the level of the bed or the gravel within.

You must always cut by hand. Never use petrol-driven or electric shears unless, I suppose, on a very large old hedge, but even then I'd hesitate. I was horrified a few years ago to see what had happened to some of the box hedges at Hidcote as a result of this treatment. When the little hedges have at last burgeoned you will find it useful to run a string along the top to get an even level but aim to learn to cut by eye. Don't worry about making mistakes. We all do and it will spring up again anyway. And do experiment. Most people just cut their parterres all to the same height bar the vertical accents. You don't have to. The hedges can be of varying heights within the same parterre and in the case of knots need to be in order to achieve the effect of interlacing. Remember that the little hedges can also be rounded. If you look at any parterre abroad you will notice that they often are but it is seldom done in England. And don't only stick in the Merrie Englande syndrome, everything having to be an eternal pastiche of Tudor knots and baroque parterres. At the moment in the large Yew Garden I've got two central parterres which are purely historicist but around the edges a whole mass of box has gone in, which I intend to clip in a strictly twentieth-century way once it gets established. It will be treated Cubist style, asymmetrical angular surfaces like those in a Picasso painting from that period.

And don't forget when you're snipping that cuttings can keep you in box for the rest of your life. It is astonishingly easy to root. The best time is August I'm told, but I've done it earlier and later. Just take the clippings, strip off the lower leaves, dip the base in hormone rooting powder and plant them in rows about three inches apart. I do this in the vegetable garden, if my wife allows me a patch. In about two years' time with feeding you'll have a bushy little plant saving you a fortune, so there's no excuse not to start snipping now.

GARDEN PLANTS

I've never considered myself a plantsman: I'm always drawn far more to the overall effect of a garden rather than to tunnel vision focusing on this or that plant. But there's not much, in fact, that cannot be learnt by actually looking, or from books. I envy those with horticultural and botanical training, but as I was taught early on in life that an educated mind could apply itself in any direction I have never been afraid of just doing precisely that and hoping for the best. And the challenge of having to write about plants for a newspaper column became the most glorious excuse to learn.

My garden library is substantial but I have to admit largely on design and history, whereas the section on plants can't run to more than about a hundred and fifty books, a drop in the ocean in plant book terms. But I can boast subsections on trees, roses and herbs. The dictionaries published by the Royal Horticultural Society are of course my plant gospels. What would we all do without them, doubly so in an age which permits lavish colour pictures to aid our ignorance. But what such books fail to give is what interests me most about a plant: its history and its potential in terms of placing within the garden. I never cease to be fascinated by the cultural context of plants, when and how they arrived, fluctuations in fashion, and their appearance in the literature of an age.

In this respect it is striking how ill-informed the average gardener is. Someone who would be quite capable of dating a house or a piece of furniture would seize up at the thought of patrolling the garden casting out a date and place of origin for its contents. Old varieties always give me a *frisson*. The botanical garden at Leiden has tulips planted in date sequence, for example, and I still recall the thrill when the custodian of England's national collection of pinks nonchalantly gestured towards one and said, 'Henry VIII would have known that.'

SNOWDROPS

One recent January we went to a Galanthus Gala. It took place at the Royal Horticultural College in Cirencester, Gloucestershire, and at the time I couldn't imagine who would turn up for such a thing. In that I was proved to be quite wrong. *Galanthus*, I might add at this juncture, is the Latin for snowdrop, a flower which has a particularly electrifying effect on some gardeners. The poor College when we arrived was already under siege and the reason was that various nurseries had already set up their snowdrop stalls in its corridors. Each was banked with a dazzling display of rare varieties but, alas, an embargo had been imposed on buying until the clock struck a particular hour. The galanthus groupies, or galanthophiles as they're known, paced the passages like predators seeing their prey but denied it. When the curfew was at last lifted all hell broke loose as they seized whatever was missing from their own particular collection. Those who saw their prey snatched before their eyes could only conceal their fury.

I've never come up against anything quite like snowdrop madness. My wife's miserable garnering of just over thirty varieties was as nothing to those groupies boasting sixty or more. What set us off on the galanthus trail was an old gentleman called Mr Bishop who lived in a cottage on a hilltop not so far from us. Over a decade ago we visited that cottage garden in late winter and were enchanted by the trickles of snowy flowers. He asked my wife whether she would like some and not long after he came to our garden with a box full 'in the green' as they say, as they must be when planted. Each was carefully labelled. They included common ones like the stately *Galanthus* 'Atkinsii' and *G. nivalis* 'Flore pleno' as well as rarer varieties like 'Mighty Atom' and 'Hill Poë'. This I now know was a more than generous gift, for many I saw figured in snowdrop catalogues at between three and six pounds a bulb. But it was, one realised, the passing on of a passion. As I took him round our garden he spoke of the death of his wife and his own followed not long after. I then knew that he had chosen his snowdrop heirs, ones who would not betray the inheritance.

That collection was well placed in my wife's hands. She planted the bulbs with care, seeing that each was meticulously labelled. Not a bulb was allowed to be naturalised either, until it had well and truly multiplied. Neat plans of her successive snowdrop beds are kept in a file alongside a photographic inventory. All of this could have been signs of an incipient galanthophile, but mercifully that hasn't happened.

There's still so much to learn about snowdrops. Some months before Christmas, someone surprised us by saying his snowdrops were in bloom already. Now I know that must have been *Galanthus reginae-olgae*, a rare one which flowers from September through till Christmas. Another one which should flower before Christmas is *G. graecus*. Ours only peep forth soon after the festive season, *G.* 'Atkinsii' in January followed by *G. nivalis*, the common snowdrop, and the heavier double form, *G. nivalis* 'Flore Pleno', which will take us through into March. Our great glory is a short walk through a shrubbery carpeted with them. Sunk beneath a luscious tapestry of leaf mould they just love it there. But we've extended the effect, for snowdrops, being over before leaves appear on deciduous trees and shrubs, are wonderful for casting a necklace of winter bloom around a plant which will later spring into leaf, giving the resting snowdrop bulb all the shade it needs in summer.

The bill wallops up with snowdrops but five of each of the varieties I've named so far will see you well on your way. And do remember that they have to be planted apart, for they quietly multiply and *G. nivalis* in particular is a rabid self-seeder, producing seedlings which will flower within three years. It is in fact amazing how short a time it takes to get a snowy carpet. Thinning them out and replanting every three years is also a great hastener of that effect.

I have to confess that although we're not groupies, they do exert a pull. The reason is simple. They are so very early and that means we do look at them with an intense observation of botanical detail which we would not apply to them if they popped up in June. But then remember that apart from the common snowdrop, you are filling your garden with rarities which deserve every bit of the attention that you pay them. Dusting the ground in autumn with bonemeal, and a dose of compost around the clumps in spring, will bring rich rewards to lighten the next winter months. Who knows, but there are worse fates in life than to become a galanthophile.

—❖—

WALLFLOWERS

The pressure's on. 'When are you going to plant out those wallflowers?' my wife petitions. I stare at one of her small raised kitchen garden beds jammed with the poor plants screaming to be moved and given space to breathe and grow. This is one of September's chores, or earlier if you like, if it's damp enough, that is, to move things. The great thing to remember, as Julia always does, is to sow the seed in springtime. Otherwise it's down to the garden centre.

No seed catalogue is complete without its listing of *Cheiranthus cheiri* (now called *Erysimum cheiri*). I'm looking at the seed packets of varieties we've grown over the last few years: 'Fire King', 'Blood Red', 'Primrose Bedder', 'Ivory White' and 'Scarlet Bedder'. But the one Julia understandably plumps for is Sutton's 'Persian Carpet' which, as the catalogue states, is a compendium 'of the most beautiful colours seen in Persian carpets including cream, apricot, rose, purple and gold'. As a pair of, on the whole, designer, rather than plantsman, gardeners, such a choice is explicable and the results have never failed us. Each springtime for nearly three months running from March to May, the flower heads give birth to all the colours that I can recall in carpets seen in places like the great mosques of Istanbul. Their colours evoke visits to spice markets with sacks heavy with the yellows, oranges, browns and ochres of turmeric, cinnamon, saffron and nutmeg.

We now find books dedicated to gardening with 'antique flowers' but surely most gardens are made up of precisely those? Going to my garden library the earliest picture I can find of an English wallflower is in a manuscript dated 1585 in the British Museum. It occurs among the botanical drawings of the Huguenot artist Jacques le Moyne de Morgues, the man who depicted the New World plants of the Elizabethan explorers. Here's our wallflower with a welcome butterfly and an unwelcome snail in attendance. The flowers are single, white and yellow. They were of the kind that the cavalier Sir Thomas Hanmer, who retreated to his garden in the dire days of the Commonwealth, wrote, 'grow usually upon old castle or stone walls', where they can still be encountered. They were known as wall gillyflowers, although they were also cultivated in gardens. 'The sweetnesse of the flowers causeth them to be generally used in Nosegayes, and to decke up houses,' wrote the herbalist John Parkinson approvingly. Today these are classified along with what in the past was regarded as quite a different plant, the stock gillyflower, and in these I recognise our Persian carpet variety. Parkinson has a down on the stock gillyflower: 'Divers have no good scent, others little or no beauty.' Ignore him, for here we have all those lovely colours, crimsons, purples, reds, whites and yellows, including doubles and singles both streaked and spotted.

But to return to where I started. My trug is full, several times over, I fear, with this Persian carpet harvest. Where to plant my evocation of Tudor and Stuart England? A few at least we always put into containers to join the tableau outside the garden door, where they will provide a welcome, even on a sunless day. Remember to pot them in indifferent soil for they don't like a rich one. And remember, too, that they love sun and good drainage. Next they are stuck willy-nilly into a bank which we look out upon from our dining-room window, so that we can enjoy the tapestry of colour at breakfast and lunch. In both cases these are early garden encounters in springtime and wallflowers offer, in sharp contrast to other spring flowers, an exotic strength of heady perfume, unmatched until the advent of flowers like lilies later in the season.

The main planting, however, will be quite a step away from the house in a garden which resides around a small cottage. There behind low walls of shiny green box they will be marshalled in their time-honoured Victorian role as bedding plants, often married with forget-me-nots or the contrasting precision of tulips. But here they will look across to tiny beds planted with Kauffmanniana tulips. This will provide a pleasant springtime walk to a hidden delight. And, as always, there'll be a few which just don't get moved from that kitchen garden. But who cares? Their fragrance and pretty colours will lighten the senses as the purple-sprouting broccoli is picked.

ACANTHUS

I'm ashamed to admit that, until the summer of 1997, I'd never clapped eyes on the Acropolis. In a way, after the event, I never wished to again but, pushing my way up through the teeming hordes, everywhere my eye fell there was that queen of decorative plants, *Acanthus mollis*, growing virtually wild. Majestic is the only word that can be applied to it, with its large thrusting lanceate leaves, shiny dark green, deeply indented into the repeating rhythms of shape, which were to provide the fount for architectural decoration for thousands of years. The strong sun of the Mediterranean enhances those latent sculptural qualities which, under the softer light of northern skies, are inevitably somewhat muted. Looking at the leaves in Greece, the leap to the Corinthian capital is not such a large one. Corinthian is the grandest of all the classical orders and the burst of formalised leaves which make up the capital approximates to the reality of the plant far more than one would at first glance think.

You have to be patient with acanthus. It takes a long time to get going, or so I've found. Ours originated from my parents-in-law's garden in Putney, London, eventually coming to rest in The Laskett flower garden and now forming quite a large suckering clump. But I have to admit that it has taken a decade to get to that, even though it's planted in the sandy soil of the kind it prefers. I could have learned that from John Parkinson, who, writing in 1629, begins a sentence on acanthus with the phrase: 'After this plant hath stood long in one place, and well defended from the injury of the cold it sendeth forth from among the leaves one or more great and strong stalkes . . .' You have been warned! And its success must also be linked to that bastion of yew hedging behind which it shelters from the devastating chill that can blast from the nearby Black Mountains which divide us from Wales.

None the less, this is a plant well worth waiting for, one of those bold architectural statements that are the mainstays of any successful border, its large jagged leaves forming the perfect foil to the floriferous froth which surrounds it, in our case bright red poppies in early summer followed by orange hemerocallis. In spring the fronds thrust upwards and unfurl and then, in midsummer, spires of flower reaching up to five feet in height follow. These are stately columns flecked with white but overall tinged with imperial purple. They're ideal for drying and we've had a vase full of some which still look handsome even after two decades.

A few years ago Rosemary Verey presented us with some *Acanthus spinosus,* which the books tell me is finer and flowers more abundantly, but that has yet to prove itself. The leaves are far more deeply indented, like exotic paper sculpture.

The plant dictionaries in fact list up to thirty species of acanthus, including recommending *Acanthus hungaricus* as the best for garden culture. In this country it seems to have been introduced by the Romans. It was certainly known in the twelfth century, when it was listed by Alexander Neckam, Abbot of Cirencester, among the 140 species of plant available to the medieval gardener. Four centuries later John Gerard gives it its old name of *Branke ursine* and refers to even older ones, Cutberdole and Cutbertill. William Turner in his *The Names of Herbes*, published in 1548, tells us that it was part of the Tudor garden flower repertory and that 'in the greatest plenty I ever saw it, I did see it in my Lord Protector's Grace's garden at Syon,' my lord being Edward VI's Duke of Somerset. By the Elizabethan period, it assumed the well-known name of bear's breeches, still used by Philip Miller in his *Gardener's Dictionary* in the middle of the eighteenth century, which describes it as 'fit for large gardens'. I would guess that it went out of fashion during the Victorian bedding-out period and came back in with William Robinson and Gertrude Jekyll. In the case of the former, it figures in his chapter on 'Beauty of Form in the Flower

Garden' in his *The English Flower Garden* and Jekyll uses it in the way we do today, as a bold architectural exclamation mark which cannot be ignored in the rhythm of any border.

I think Miller got it right when he wrote that it is a plant for quite large gardens. It needs space, an area not less than about five feet square, for it to make its impact to any advantage. Unless the winter is exceptionally severe its highly decorative gothic leaves will go through those months giving interest to an otherwise empty flower border – a point in its favour. Once it has got going, it calls for little attention beyond stopping it spreading. As in the case of so many plants, I love it as much for its resonances through time as for its reality.

ROSES

'A rose is a rose is a rose . . .' Well, for how much longer I don't know, as rose gardens are passing more and more out of fashion. Our so-called Rose Garden now only has eight half-standards which float a froth of white petals above an ocean of lime-green *Alchemilla mollis* and spikes of deep purple 'Hidcote' lavender spilling over clipped box. It was far otherwise when I first planted it in 1974. Then, my old rose period, it was crammed with over thirty, with everything from the beautiful white Damask 'Mme Hardy' to the Bourbon pale pink striped with lilac mauve 'Honorine de Brabant'. Roses are beginner's plants. They grow quickly and provide instant bloom. Only later do the drawbacks of pruning, their susceptibility to every form of weird disease and the fleeting nature of their bloom impinge on one's consciousness. A dazzling month at the most and then that's it.

But I fell in love with them as much for their names and associations as anything else. They formed a kind of horticultural *Almanach de Gotha*. Who was the Duchesse de Montebello, let alone the Comtesse de Murinais? And then there were those truly historic roses like York and Lancaster (now called *R. × damascena* var. *versicolor*), blooms striped in crimson and white, known to have existed when those two great dynasties stained the field of battle with blood. Roses, almost more than any other plants, are endowed with all the resonances of history. The fact that so many are named after people endows them for me with a touching humanity. Lord Penzance, Lady Waterlow, Louise Odier, Docteur Jamain and Ferdinand Picard fill the garden with old friends. How lucky to live on as a rose.

At present there are some sixty different types of rose – not that many scattered over our four acres. One fact emerges loud and clear: there is not one planted which is not part of a garden picture which stands on its own without the rose. It might bring a moment of luscious high drama for a fleeting week or two, but when it has gone there is no sense of a gap, of a yawning void until next summer comes around. The temple is flanked by 'Paul's Himalayan Musk' and 'Veilchenblau' which, when in flower, offer a floriferous culmination, the former's pale lemon blooms now engulfing a weeping silver birch, but they're preceded by *Clematis montana* 'Elizabeth' and in the autumn there's a claret-coloured *Vitis coignetiae*. And the trellis they are trained on to is painted blue, interesting to look at in its own right. In the

Birthday Garden there's a snowstorm of 'Wickwar', quite incredible for a very brief period, embracing pillars of salmon-pink 'Compassion', a modern climber that repeat flowers until late in the season. In the orchard there are Rugosas, *Rosa roxburghii* and 'Fru Dagmar Hastrup', gorgeous flowers and splendid hips, but there are spring flowers and blossom before and fruit for the autumn. Some balustrading is festooned gracefully with Wichuranas, 'May Queen' and one of my favourites, 'Albéric Barbier', but when they're over, moss and lichen-enriched stonework takes the eye. The moral seems to be: don't plant a rose anywhere in a garden that isn't interesting in its own right without it in the first place.

Rose books are forever telling you that roses are wonderful for hiding something ugly. They're not. I have two pretty roses scrabbling up a hideous hut masking the oil tank and a couple of dustbins. For a period the eye is slightly distracted by this *pointilliste* display of pink and crimson and then there it is back again, that horrendous clapped-out shed. Remember, a rose can embellish a garden feature which is pleasant to look at, but hide it never.

So it's not surprising that I've ended up with a rose garden virtually without a rose. Treated as one other source of bloom in the garden's design, roses have proved far more satisfactory. Standards, which I used to view as suburban 1930s, I now look on in a new light. I've planted brilliant yellow ones called 'Sun Hit' in a large box parterre, perfect symmetrical vertical accents bringing colour floating like a sunburst against the dark green of the containing yew hedge. In summer, the beds below are filled with African marigolds in shades of crushed orange, ochre and brown velvet. Into the flower border I've tucked more standards just pell-mell, where I think flowers can float above yet more flowers beneath. These are the normal standard height, three feet three inches, but some of the prettiest effects can be got with the new half-standards budded at two feet six inches above the ground. That puts their flowering head just over the average height of the floral waterline of most foreground planting. 'Kent', with pure white double blooms, is in the so-called Rose Garden, and bluish-pink 'Avon' provides verticals in a tiny cottage garden, each rose rising from a pattern of clipped box balls. They are remarkably disease resistant and provide continuous bloom from early June through to October. I can't recommend them enough.

SWEET PEAS

I have an affection for sweet peas, *Lathyrus odoratus*, not that I've grown them, but I'm beginning to think that we should. So often one is put off by one's earliest encounters with a plant. Every year on my wife's birthday, the cottager who loyally fed our cat when we were away used to come up the drive with a bunch of them. They scented the house for days and Julia adored them, but I always remember passing his little garden and seeing the trenching and staking that had gone on to produce this annual floral feast. Not, I thought, flowers for the hard-pressed gardener. So they've belonged to that garden category which is headed by 'borrowed landscape', that is something which you don't own or do yourself but enjoy at someone else's expense and labour. In the case of sweet peas, they are generally savoured peeping over a wall or hedge in passing, in our case on the outskirts of Cirencester, where every year a small row of cane wigwams sprouts like soldiers on parade in springtime to be garlanded in pastel shades of pink, violet, blue, cerise and white until the frosts of October spell their death knell.

The most spectacular display of sweet peas I have ever seen was at a dinner given in the Raphael Cartoon Court of the Victoria & Albert Museum by Geoffrey Howe when he was Foreign Secretary. Every blossom from the whole of the south of England must have been felled for that floral explosion. It was only later that I came across the comment of that great Victorian plantsman E.A. Bowles, whose verdict on them as flowers for the dining table reads as follows: 'A dinner-table decorated heavily with Sweet Peas spoils my dinner, as I taste Sweet Peas with every course, and they are horrible as a sauce for fish, whilst they ruin the bouquet of good wine.' Flower arrangers please take note.

A vase of them is welcome in a guest bedroom, as we experienced the other day. Outside in the wide herbaceous borders of the garden capacious towers of twigs had been made supporting not the blooms which were in the vase, which were modern hybrids, but their ancestor, the highly perfumed *Lathyrus odoratus* which was grown up until the beginning of this century.

Now there's a great deal of snobbery about sweet peas. The original variety produce highly scented flowers in shades of white, red, pink and blue. I recall when I was filming at Highgrove a few years back, the Prince of Wales and Lady Salisbury hymning what they referred to as the pre-Spencer varieties as if the poor sweet pea had formed a misalliance with a kitchen maid. Vita Sackville-West, who writes as though she had swum the Channel with the horticultural *Almanach de Gotha* between her teeth, similarly has a down on the modern hybrids. These, with their frilled petals, first appeared in the garden of Countess Spencer at Althorp at the beginning of this century and they're what most people grow. You have to watch out that they retain the scent of their ancestor, but even Vita admits that the modern varieties are sturdier, have more flower heads and a wider colour range. So *chacun à son goût*.

Accounts of how the sweet pea got here are confusing. It is a native of southern Italy and Sicily and its arrival is attributed to seeds sent by a Father Cupani in 1699 to Robert Uvedale, a great character who ran an upper class boys' school at Enfield and at the same time maintained one of the earliest hot-houses in the country. 'His flowers', it is recorded, 'are choice, his stock numerous, and his culture of them methodical and curious.' Two decades later the botanist Thomas Fairchild was recommending that sweet peas were planted in London squares on account not only of their beauty but also of their smell, which was 'something like honey, and a little tending to orange flower smell'. The architect Sir William Chambers was making use of them for his shrub borders in the 1770s and by the close of the century the sweet pea was a standard ingredient of what was a revival of the flower garden. In a rare plan of a circular island bed at Hartwell House in 1799 there is the sweet pea. And it didn't sink from favour during the Victorian era, William Robinson in *The Flower Garden* referring to it as 'perhaps the most precious annual plant grown'.

Where does this leave me as I look at the lurid pages of the seed catalogues which tell me there is a National Sweet Pea Society? I'm pleased to see that the pre-Spencer varieties can still be obtained, labelled Edwardian Collection or Old-fashioned Varieties but for their descendants the drive is as always for larger flowers and stronger colour, although scent is not altogether neglected. The Bouquet Series is heralded as 'a complete rethink in sweet pea breeding', whatever that means. But with all that demand for a rich soil, a hole stuffed full of manure and compost plus the staking, maybe I'll remain peering at them over the garden fence and leave them for the enthusiast.

MARIGOLDS

Outside the back door leading to the garden my wife always masses containers, so that no matter what the season of the year, there's a bloom to welcome me every time I step out into the garden. In summer many are filled with pot marigolds, *Calendula*, sunbursts of vibrant orange and buttery yellow which will go on blooming well into October, until the first severe frosts of autumn begin to wither them. These are flowers which epitomise the garden as collective memory, ones which stretch back across time to the sparse planting of a medieval monastic herber, or a Tudor knot. They remind us, too, that flowers in the past had a symbolic as well as a botanical significance, a lost way of looking. The French king Henri IV's mother, the pious Marguerite, Queen of Navarre, had as her emblem a marigold with its face turned to the sun, a message that her thoughts were ever heavenwards. That obedience is caught in popular names like Summer's Bride or Husbandman's Dyall. Perdita, in a well-known line from *The Winter's Tale*, refers to the habit:

The marigold, that goes to bed with the sun,
And with him rises weeping: these are flowers
Of middle summer.

They are fit, she says, to be given to middle-aged men but why I know not. By the nineteenth century, when they were looked down upon as being somewhat common, they signified grief in the Victorian language of flowers.

We've always planted them. One year I infilled beds of lavender with marigolds, producing an unforgettable spectacle of rich purple and deepest orange-gold offset against shiny containing walls of green clipped box and sombre yew. I never hesitate to pop a few, raised by my wife in the kitchen garden from seed, into a gap in a border alongside any blue or purple flowers, although, on account of their strength of colour, they're at their singing best alone with greens. That is why they always look right in the kitchen garden cheering up the vegetables, whose differences are ones of contrasting habit and leaf shape and not of colour. There they are free to wander for, by nature, as summer draws ever onward, they tend to lose their upright stance and contentedly relax and meander. Marigolds are one of those flowers which start the season tidy and end up all over the place, but who cares, for as autumn takes its toll, one is glad of the odd sunny flower face to cheer a lustreless day. Mrs

Earle sums it up in *Pot-pourri from a Surrey Garden* when, as late as 28 October, she trots down her kitchen garden taking in her patch of self-sown marigolds: 'As they proudly defy early frost, they become really precious with their grand glowing orange faces . . . No garden, however small, should be without this patch devoted to Marigolds.'

The furry and at times almost sticky quality of their stems and leaves I have to admit to finding unattractive. It's odd that such a beguiling and pretty flower should lack a more engaging tactile quality. But otherwise marigolds are no-nonsense plants, happy to grow in the poorest of soil as long as it's sunny. Every seed catalogue has them and once they are established you can save the seedheads, as we have often done, for next year's planting. If you need to take their height into consideration remember that they come in short and tall varieties, about one foot as against two. We've grown 'Orange King', one of the tall varieties with knock-out, almost top-heavy orange flowers, and also two shorter varieties, the early flowering 'Yellow Gitana' and the compact 'Fiesta Gitana' which sports a kaleidoscope of double flowers in oranges and golds. And, unlike most packets of seeds these days, they are generously filled.

For the first-time gardener, few flowers offer such an encouraging introduction to the delights of annuals, for they germinate quickly as long as you keep them watered. Aphid and mildew will take their toll, but don't let that deter you. Always remember that these are joyous flowers. Just the sight of them makes me feel happy. And remember, too, that the flowers are edible, although I've not myself gone beyond scattering a few petals to make the contents of an otherwise dull salad bowl sparkle. The taste is bitter and peppery, adding piquancy. Dorothy Hartley, in her classic *Food in England* (1996), gives a recipe for marigold cheese, which was traditionally made in August or September and which perhaps someone might be brave enough to revive.

Then there's their role as a cut flower. In Vienna you can still see tiny almost incandescent posies of marigolds tied up with blue cornflowers in the shop windows. In this we glimpse what must be a tradition which goes back to the age of Schubert, the Biedermeier era which followed the Napoleonic wars. This was an inward-looking age centred on the home, with sparsely furnished rooms into which the light fell through lace-festooned curtains, but always the interiors would be dotted with tiny vases bearing trophies of flowers. The marigolds and cornflowers must have been like jewels set into the monochrome. In Scandinavia you can also glimpse marigolds, this time great explosions of them bunched in zinc buckets in florists' shops, reminders that in countries where the winters are really hard, the brightness of the humble calendula bestows a special gladness. So do plant some.

DAHLIAS

To misquote Vita Sackville-West on another despised flower, the lobelia, I would like to put in a good word for the dahlia. Poor dahlia. It has been the victim of horticultural disdain for far too long. Russell Page may sing its praises and Christopher Lloyd dig up his rose garden at Great Dixter to replant it with dahlias, but even the voices of these greatest of gardening gurus are like cries in the wilderness. Somewhere along the line, the dahlia has become naff. Its name conjures up rows of staked plants bearing blooms the size of mopheads and the colour of the nastier mutilations in *Titus Andronicus*.

It wasn't always so. Shirley Hibberd, that great Victorian populariser of gardening, wrote of the dahlia: 'If regarded from the florist's point of view, it is one of the grandest flowers in the garden, and in rank must be second only to the rose.' Perhaps this is part of the problem. Dahlias are blighted by the hand of the town hall flower arranger. Hibberd was writing for the middle classes, so the dahlia had already suffered a downward social slip since its celebrated arrival from Spain in the 1790s, via the greenhouse of the Marchioness of Bute.

Looking at an individual bloom – even the more garish examples – it seems almost churlish to spurn such an incredible feat of nature. But in the very unnaturalness of its beauty lie the seeds of the dahlia's demise. The psychedelic colour, the startling geometry, the pert precision of form are out of tune with the cottagey fashions of recent years. Isn't it time for a change? Even I shall never be an *aficionado* of the most outlandish orange offenders. But to dismiss the lot is to deny yourself the pleasure of the subtler shapes and shades.

I don't know who first put the boot in for dahlias. It wasn't William Robinson, who still gives the best advice on their use – to intermingle them into the flower border. That is what I do – scattering the flowers in a garden all shades of lilac and white. Suddenly, among the Michaelmas daisies and second flush of 'Iceberg' roses, comes a garland of perfectly shaped flowers – pompons and starbursts, as well as those that explode pell mell like a sixties petal hat, graduating in hue from honey to creamy-white. Just a few, not too many, that's all I would ever want. Then, dahlias are just delectable.

Briar Roses

Over twenty years ago when we started The Laskett garden we gave over a large area to 'Lord Penzance' briars, now long since gone. That was the first time that I was entranced by the beauty of rose hips. This planting of sweet briars, I recall, included deep pink *Rosa* 'Amy Robsart', 'Anne of Geierstein' with its gold-centred crimson flowers, 'Meg Merrilies' and, of course, the one named after his lordship, both the latter variations of crimson too. I confess that I miss their apple-scented foliage but not their explosive habit, for they rampaged on a scale where a choice had to be made, us or them. But *en masse*, festooned with hips in shades of orange into scarlet and crimson, they made an unforgettable autumn spectacle caught in that soft golden light which sets autumn apart as a specially magical time of the garden year.

Those red hips gave me one of my first great lessons about autumn interest in the garden and now, as we spend our time trying somehow to perfect a more sustained cycle of seasonal interest, those rose hips have swum again into focus. One group of hip-bearing roses has been planted in the orchard interspersed between our dwarf-rooting-stock apples. That now gives us a sequence which runs spring bulbs, fruit blossom, roses in flower, then, as a finale, the fruit itself and the rose hips. And all of this unfolds against a backdrop tapestry of dark green yew. The roses here consist of *Rosa roxburghii*, of which the rosarian Peter Beales has written: 'This little group of fine shrubs deserves to be seen more often', a view to which I would subscribe. In the autumn they produce almost flask-shaped green hips curiously covered with bristles. Then there's a number of that serviceable old trooper the 'Roseraie de l'Haÿ' with its large rounded, orange-scarlet hips, hugely decorative. And the old eglantine rose, *R. rubiginosa* (syn. *R. eglanteria*) which retains its hips well into winter.

The other group is closer to the house in proximity to a large fountain. In the main these are made up of good-value Rugosas, the endlessly suckering *R.* 'Blanche Double de Coubert', *R. rugosa* 'Alba' which has quite the most astonishingly large fruits – almost resembling small tomatoes – *R. forrestiana* with long somewhat irregular hips of orange tinged into scarlet, *R.* 'Geranium' and *R. glauca*. We used to have more but they fell victim to changes in the garden's design. Looking at my annotated rose book, I can recommend 'Fru Dagmar Hastrup', *R. gymnocarpa* var. *willmottiae*, *R. woodsii* var. *fendleri*, *R. moyesii* var. *rosea* and *R.* 'Complicata'. They all, I might add, call for space, so in the case of a small garden, choose only one and place it perhaps at the back of a border. Like all roses, it will call for an evergreen backdrop to set off both flowers and hips to advantage.

I'm a bit puzzled as to when people actually began to appreciate roses for their hips and not just their flowers. It was striking that as far as I could find, hips are not dealt with in either of the two main rose gospels, *The Rose Garden* (1848) by that celebrated Victorian nurseryman, William Paul, and

Roses for English Gardens (1902) by Gertrude Jekyll and Edward Mawley. Both books are solidly focused on the flowers, understandable perhaps in the case of people who grew up in the heyday of the rose garden as an annual spectacle which was visited in June and left empty for the remainder of the year. But the hips do occur in that seminal book by Jekyll's mentor William Robinson, *The Wild Garden* (1870). There, under 'Native Briars and Wild Roses', occurs the sentence: 'There is much beauty of leaf among the plants, and variety in the quality of the fruit, some kinds being valuable for their fruit.' This is, I fancy, the fount we are looking for in their current appreciation.

That would have taken off after 1918 with the increasing planting of naturalistic wild gardens, but the real boost must finally have come in 1934 when it was discovered that the hips of English wild roses contained more vitamin C than any other fruit or vegetable. This fact became significant in the Second World War when sources of vitamin C, such as oranges, were unobtainable. Under the aegis of government, commercial manufacturers made rose hip syrup and schoolchildren in particular were sent out in droves to collect the hips as part of the war effort. Indeed my wife vividly recalls her expeditions with an aunt along the hedgerows in the country gathering the fruits.

I fancy that it is only the twentieth century that has really appreciated the fruits of the rose as against its blossom and I can't help feeling that a lot, too, must be owed to the flower arranger, Constance Spry, and her successors. The *R. glauca* with its sprays of glaucous grey-blue foliage adorned with hips, makes an elegant contribution to any autumn floral arrangement. In the face of the current trend against

QUINCES

Baked quinces, *Cydonia oblonga*, were Sir Isaac Newton's favourite pudding – a redeeming touch to an otherwise daunting man. Jane Grigson gives the recipe in her *Good Things* (1971); indeed she provides a chapter on the fruit, a splendid help to those who wonder what to do with it. In the case of Newton's pudding, all you do is wash and wipe off the furry grey bloom on the golden fruits, core them, stuff them with sugar, pop a knob of butter on the top, put them in a dish with a little water and bake them slowly. Serve them with cold cream. Delicious.

That link with the great scientist tells us that this is an ancient fruit. It went under in the Victorian age when popular taste turned to soft fruits and has only now begun, once again, to take up its rightful place in our gardens. In the Iberian peninsula and in eastern Europe it has retained it. Who knows but one day I might see a few in a supermarket. No medieval, Tudor or Stuart housewife worth her salt would have been without them, not only for making such goodies as the perennial 'faire pie of quinces' (which the Virgin Queen was partial to), but to tuck amongst the linen for their unique fragrance. And then there's the famous jelly. When the Jesuit priest John Gerard was being hounded in 1594 all he had to eat in his hiding place was 'a biscuit or two and a little quince jelly which my hostess happened to have by her and handed me as I was going in'. Lucky man.

This is a fruit to fall in love with, and indeed it came to me and to our garden through marriage. Before my wife's grandfather's house, Frewin Hall in Oxford, stood this venerable quince tree. Suckers from it went to my parents-in-law's house and its suckers, in turn, arrived at The Laskett in 1973 along with our furniture in the removal van. We never knew what variety that tree was until the Royal Horticultural Society's invaluable identification service told us that it was a Siberian quince, 'Lescovatz' from Lescovata. Since then Julia has collected some seven more varieties: 'Champion', 'Le Bourgeaut', 'Early Prolific', 'Seibosa', 'Vranja', 'Ludovic' and 'Meech's Prolific'.

By far the most famous is the Portugal quince 'Lusitanica' which the horticulturist John Parkinson, writing in 1629, describes as 'a great yellow Quince . . . this is so pleasant being fresh gathered that it may be eaten like unto an Apple without offense'. Don't believe him unless you want to have your teeth shattered. Quinces are a very hard fruit, hard work, too, to peel, but well worth the effort for their unique taste as much as for their aromatic scent.

But what about their role in the garden? These are beautiful trees. Their leaves unfold in springtime, a ravishing pale chalky grey-green, quite small and crinkled in appearance, the branches of the tree twiggy and tending to cascade downwards. There's pretty white-pink blossom but the great spectacle is the one in October into November with the fruit. This is gold of a kind normally associated with the intense yellows of the flower garden in late summer and early autumn. It is as though the branches were bedecked with lanterns for a party. Caught in autumn sunshine they are a stunning sight.

And please don't think that they are just for the orchard. I saw some in Belgium planted into the flower border – and why not? Here our use of them has proliferated. I've rescued two suckers which I'm training into decorative shrubs in tiny box-edged beds in a little cottage garden just for the pleasure of looking at them. My wife has even planted a quince hedge. These are good value, adaptable trees, full of romance and, as such, a wonderful wedding present. The ancient Greeks had a law that this fruit should be eaten at every marriage feast just before the couple retired to bed. They are totally unfussy as to the soil you plant them in and within two years they fruit and you will be able to make that memorable jelly. I will refrain from expounding the delights of quince vodka.

There's no doubt that the best variety to start off with is the historic Portugal quince, with 'Meech's Prolific' as a close second. It is the sheer size of the fruit on the Portugal quince which is so astonishing. We owe that quince to John Tradescant, gardener to Charles I's queen, Henrietta Maria, who imported the first one in 1611. Meech's we owe to a Connecticut clergyman in the early Victorian period. No matter which your choice, make sure to put one or the other on your autumn planting list.

— ❖ —

NASTURTIUMS

Tucked away in the Victoria & Albert Museum there is one of my wife's favourite flower paintings, a study by Fantin-Latour of one of the glories of any late summer garden, nasturtiums (*Tropaeolum majus*). We can only see what is the top half of a wigwam of twigs, up which the plant clambers, an eruption of oval, platter-like leaves inset with double flowers of marigold and burnt orange. All that's missing from the leaves is a scattering of glistening raindrops, something which, after a late summer shower, forms a favourite garden picture. Fantin-Latour must have taken his pot indoors to paint.

Visitors to Giverny at this time of year will know that Monet was also mad about nasturtiums, or *capucines* as they are called in French. Here they invade from either side of the wide gravelled central path, the Grande Allée, providing, at their height, an unforgettable garden spectacle of almost oriental splendour. They in fact meet in the middle, providing a vista along what can only be described as a *capucine* carpet. To achieve this, their trailing stems are only allowed to grow a yard either side on to the path and are then cut back to check any further growth and also pruned to reveal the flowers. Monet's gardens are always about joy and happiness and surely this flower was to him a symbol of just such a state of mind and of the emotions? Also, he was not inhibited by colour (what Impressionist would be?), for from one direction the orange, yellow and scarlet flowers are seen against the house painted pink, green and blue in a way which would give apoplexy to any modern good-taste gardener.

At The Laskett we've always grown nasturtiums since our

first summer here over twenty years ago, when we cultivated them for quick effect. Now they find an annual home in the kitchen garden, which is their time-honoured domain within the English tradition, for the seeds, if gathered up before they harden, used to be and indeed still can be made into capers to be used for sauce with boiled mutton. We just let the plants tumble hither and thither sprawling through the vegetables. Where they hit a plant support or a piece of trellis, up they go; otherwise they just sprawl. But they provide continuous bloom from July through until the first autumn frosts decimate their succulent stalks and foliage.

Nasturtiums, it should be remembered, can be eaten, not only the leaves but the flowers too. Pick a few leaves and toss them into the salad bowl along with your other greens and use the flowers for a pretty garnish. I remember once making a delicious mushroom and nasturtium bake, layered like a gratin. A mid-Victorian gardening dictionary on my shelves records: 'The flowers are used to garnish dishes, particularly by artificial light . . .' That must have been written in the gas age and the writer was looking back to earlier in the century when the yellows and oranges would have sung out in the candlelight on many a Regency dining table.

The earliest nasturtiums came from Mexico or Peru in the late sixteenth century by way of Spain. They'd already reached England in the Elizabethan period, when they are recorded in the herbalist John Gerard's garden. He was clearly wildly excited about 'this Beautiful Plant' and explains how 'seeds of this rare and faire plant came from the Indies into Spaine, and thence into France and Flanders, from whence I received seed that bore with mee both floures and seed . . .' He reproduces a woodcut of it but there's an even better picture of this early form amongst the watercolours in Alexander Marshal's flower album in the Royal Collection, painted in the middle of the next century. By then, John Rea in his *Flora* (1676) takes the nasturtium for granted as a garden flower 'so well known that I need not be curious in describing it'. Then it was called Indian cress or 'yellow Larks-heels'. The plant we see in Marshal's album was about to become a museum piece, for a decade later the ancestor of our present varieties arrived. This is the plant which was grown in the gardens of William III and in eighteenth-century flower gardens. Towards the end of that century a double variety came in.

Today any catalogue contains seeds of the Gleam, Jewel and Whirlybird Series. All of them have a colour range running through crimson, salmon, orange, cerise, yellow and other golden shades; their habits are various – early or late flowering, some offering more or larger blooms and some more compact plants as against those whose trailing propensities range from the rampant to a frond polite enough for dangling from a hanging basket. They're such easily grown plants, happy, as long as they have sun, to thrive in rather poor soil. If you have not planted any think about doing so next year. To my eyes they are at their best precisely if positioned to erupt across an area, adding a tangled mass of colour where it is needed late in the season. They are wonderful wandering across paving close to the house or indeed any hard surface which faces south and is warm and sunny. Start them off near to any containing balustrading, screening or trellis up which they can climb and then they will spill over, trailing their Impressionist palate as they advance at your feet in delight.

GARLIC

By August we've harvested our garlic for the year. Be warned: take no notice of books on vegetable growing which tell you that only a few plants need be grown, as a single clove is usually sufficient to add a distinctive flavour to a dish. Speaking as the cook, I preside over a kitchen which positively devours garlic. I only have to think of that recipe in which a chicken is pot-roasted on a bed of forty cloves, let alone the dozen or more I sprinkle over a pan of roasted mixed vegetables tossed in virgin olive oil and chopped rosemary. Then there's aïoli, not to mention the extraordinary Persian pickled garlic which my wife makes. And have you tried roasting whole heads of it, dribbled with olive oil, and then squeezing the creamy garlic on to bread and eating it with roast lamb? The truth is you can't have enough of it.

Always remember that the best place to buy the garlic you are going to plant is *not* England. I recall vividly our strolling along the Quai des Fleurs in Paris, with its plant and seed shops sprawling across the pavements, and alighting for the first time on the three classic varieties: *blanc*, *rose* and *violet*, each recognisable by the colour which faintly tinges its papery outer skin. *L'ail rose* is the one which lasts the longest, with luck until next season's young bulbs are ready to harvest. Leave them for up to three months in warm air if you can, with their stalks on but out of direct sunlight. Ours are slung up into the rafters of our dilapidated garage on hammocks made of wire mesh. Later in the autumn, before the frosts come, they are tied into bunches and brought into the house for use during the winter months and into the spring.

Violet and *blanc* are slightly larger than *rose*, but we've grown them all, plus an American form of elephant garlic which we came across, unexpectedly labelled, in a supermarket. Strangely no such sophistication in terms of selling different varieties seems to have yet penetrated our island. Garlic is merely garlic on the supermarket shelves, which is why I counsel purchasing some in a market abroad during the summer holidays and bringing it back to plant. And when it comes to that moment I cannot stress enough the importance of getting the cloves into the soil by the close of September or early October at the latest. Plant them two inches deep and about ten inches apart. There is, of course, a danger that green shoots will appear and be frostbitten, but always take that chance. The longer garlic is in the soil, the better. We're lucky, our soil is made for members of the allium family. It is light and well drained. Garlic needs sun, but otherwise it requires no tending; just leave it until the leaves wither to brown, when it should be gathered into store.

Garlic is not, I admit, very exciting in terms of looks. If it goes to seed the flowerheads are somewhat disappointing. But grow it for what it is, a culinary staff of life. Thankfully the days are long gone when the mere mention of it was almost a breach of etiquette. From the Victorian period until the age of Elizabeth David, who reformed English cookery after the Second World War, its use had to be covert. The idea of a trace of its pungency being left on the breath was anathema. Poor Mrs McKee, the plain up-and-down cook who ministered to the present queen when she was a princess, was told two things: one was to curtsy, the other never to use garlic.

It has taken decades for us to recover the fact that it is not a foreign vegetable but part of our indigenous tradition, written about by our earliest herbalists. Not that garlic didn't have its problems in the past. It was out of favour with the ancient Greeks and Romans. Indeed the Greeks made criminals eat it for several days to cleanse them from their crime. We owe its introduction to England to the Romans, who in the end took it into their kitchens. In the Middle Ages it was an important medicinal preventative, a clove being held in the mouth to ward off plague. Indeed its use ranged over a whole bizarre scenario of remedies, from being an antidote to dog bites to acting as a deterrent against vampires for virgins. Today it is valued as a control of cholesterol levels and unbelievably a recent statistic showed that more garlic was consumed in the south of England than in the entire of northern France.

But, to come back to gardening, there is no evidence that that statistic would be matched by a similar one for the growing of it. In most people's minds garlic is still viewed as something exotic and continental, a vegetable to be popped into the supermarket trolley along with root ginger or grapefruit. The truth of the matter is that garlic is an honourable British vegetable grown here for hundreds of years until exiled by etiquette. Indeed it appears in our earliest herbal, that by Thomas Tusser published in 1548, where it is described as a plant 'which groweth in gardines onely'. So there really is no excuse for you not to plant a large bed of it next autumn.

MEDLARS

My wife has a passion for medlar trees *(Mespilus germanica)*. In fact we have recently even planted what we hope to train into a medlar tunnel. Others are scattered along the drive up to the garage and into the orchard, but the two most handsomely sited flank a fountain and are part of quite a complex formal composition. In a way this represents a progression from collecting what is a curiosity among fruit trees to realising that here is a real enrichment to any garden's visual delights. Forget the fruit, which I'll come to, and just remember that in the late autumn the medlar changes colour like no other fruit tree. It can hold its own even against the most opulent of the acers. And it is that fact which explains their graduation in our garden, to use a theatrical turn of phrase, from back to front of house. The two which flank the fountain arise from clipped hedges of deepest purple berberis like flames erupting from a volcano, when touched by sunlight incandescent in shades of deepest gold, ochre, orange, crimson and burnt sienna. Then in November the leaves fall, leaving the fruit as decoration on the branches.

Medlars were certainly appreciated just for being beautiful in the Middle Ages, the author of the mid-fifteenth-century poem *The Flower and the Leaf* writing:

> I was ware of the fairest medlar tree
> That ever yet in all my life I see,
> As full of blossom as it might be.

That blossom comes late, towards the end of May or June, hence avoiding frosts. The flowers are white or slightly pinkish in colour, attractive on a tree whose shape, with its gnarled and twisted trunk, spells antiquity. There's a beguiling ungainliness to the medlar but it's a tree which, if you choose to plant it, never fails to attract people's attention.

Before the last century no garden would have been without one and indeed they used to, and indeed may still, grow wild in some parts of the country. In one recent tree book they're referred to as trees from a bygone age which one might just find in some old cottage garden. The Victorian age sealed their fate. William Cobbett gave the poor medlar a perfectly horrible press: 'A very poor thing ... It is hardly worth notice, at best, only one degree better than a rotten apple.' I have eaten the fruit and don't care that much for it, I must admit, but then our attitude to the fruit is the same as that to flowers: it is just beautiful to look at. Curious and strange are two words that cross the mind. Primitive is another, appropriate to what is an odd-shaped fruit which has an end indented with the seed vessels visible in the eye. Around the run of the indentation stand five conspicuous calyx lobes. Once one has seen them, one understands why William Turner, the herbalist, refers in 1548, to the medlar as the 'Open ars tree' and the French, equally uncomplimentary, as *cul de chien*.

But don't let that put you off! We have four varieties: 'Nottingham', which is the one most easily obtainable and whose fruit is smallish; 'Dutch', which has a somewhat weeping habit; and two others which bear larger fruit, 'Large Dutch' and 'Monstrous' John Parkinson refers to the 'greater and lesser English' and the 'Nepolitan'. (It is now thought that the 'greater English' is in fact 'Dutch', and the 'lesser' is probably 'Nottingham'.) John Evelyn, in his *Sylva*, also refers to the 'Nepolitan' but goes on to the 'Great Dutch' and one other 'without Stones'. Beware those stones. They can break the blades of a blender.

If you choose to eat the fruits you must gather them in November when they are just going soft, store them, calyx-side down, on newspaper on trays, and wait until they are 'blet', a euphemism for verging on rotten. They are not an elegant fruit to eat as one is reduced to more or less sucking the soft pulp out of the skin. The invaluable Jane Grigson in her *Fruit Book* (1982) describes a visit to the Bibliothèque Nationale in search of the medlar and learning of its surprising medicinal qualities: it is recommended to be taken against looseness and eaten by women to avoid haemorrhages. Apparently a chemical analysis of 1939 demonstrated that the medlar was a perfect regulator of the stomach.

What we do make from time to time is medlar jelly, superb with any meat like lamb or game which is complimented by a tart fruit jelly. Jane Grigson gives an excellent recipe which calls for two to one of well 'bletted' medlars as against those which are soft yet still firm. Cover them with water and boil them until the fruit is soft. Strain off the liquid and then boil with sugar, a pound to a pint of liquid, until setting point is reached. The colour is quite indescribably beautiful in the jar, translucent amber. Potted up prettily they make wonderful house gifts and Christmas presents. But I must stress that we'd grow the tree regardless of that, just for the sheer pleasure that it always gives.

HOLLY

There was holly in the field hedges at The Laskett when we came here. It remains there still, although the hedges have since been sculpted, the one up the drive into swags, the other along the road allowed to soar upwards and its leaders trained into pompons. Where we took out an old field hedge we hadn't the heart to cut down the holly. Instead I topiarised it. There it still incongruously stands, somewhat, I admit, in the way. As far as I know, it is just common English holly, *Ilex aquifolium*.

At that early stage I didn't plant any holly, in a sense put off by warnings as to its dilatory growth, and also by moving some self-seeded ones which promptly died on me. It wasn't until a decade later that I came to terms with this beautiful evergreen. Rosemary Verey suddenly presented me with four plants of *Ilex* × *altaclerensis* 'Golden King', a compact shrub with large leaves grey-green at the centre but richly dappled with an almost luminous gold at the edges. At her famous garden at Barnsley, she had beautifully sited some as corner sentinels to her two knot gardens.

Plant gifts, as all gardeners know, produce agony as well as ecstasy. Ecstasy at the generosity, agony over whatever to do with it. At the time I had just made a flower garden to learn about flowers ('About time too,' she remarked), and I was concerned as to how one was to maintain any interest during the winter months in what would otherwise have been just a dead area. In the Victorian period, I recalled, it was customary after the bedding-out plants had been ripped up to fill the flower beds with an arrangement of evergreens. These were lifted out each spring and planted in store, as it were, during the summer months. That is a luxury which few can run to today, but it gave me the idea as to where to dispose of my hollies. Into the flower garden they went, to be trained into cushions and standards alongside clipped box balls and topiary verticals in yew.

When I walk around the garden on any winter day they now fill me with rapture. On a sun-touched one, they light up the beds, clipped mounds of gold radiating warmth. In the summer they are virtually invisible, lost beneath the cornucopia of foliage and flower of the border. So I've become a holly convert. We've in fact just planted a low yew hedge interspersed with what I intend to train into holly cakestands running along a walk over sixty yards in length. They are common English holly and arrived containerised.

It's such an English plant, the holly. I think of the poet Robert Herrick's lines in the aftermath of Christmas: 'Down with holly, down with bays', or the fate of poor John Evelyn's celebrated holly hedge at Sayes Court, Deptford, Kent. The diarist had let his house to Czar Peter the Great and a perverted sense of fun had led the Czar to be pushed through the hedge in a wheelbarrow. Poor Evelyn was devastated by what he found. It stuck in his mind when he wrote his well-known eulogy of the virtues of holly: 'Is there under Heaven a more glorious and refreshing Object of the kind than an impregnable Hedge of about four hundred foot in length, nine feet high and five in diameter; which I can show in my now ruin'd Gardens (thanks to the Czar of Muscovy) at any time of the Year, glitt'ring with its arm'd and varnish'd leaves?' Quite so.

A holly hedge is a long-term but worthwhile investment. Hollies are splendid in the shrubbery and, if your garden is small, clip one into a shape. Cut it in summer. The plant dictionaries list a daunting four hundred varieties with variations in leaf-formation and colour as well as the colour of the berries. I personally don't warm to those with cream or silver-edged leaves, like *Ilex aquifolium* 'Silver Queen', as they visually chill. I'd always plump for those etched and splodged with yellow, some with leaves just chastely outlined like *Ilex altaclerensis* 'Belgica Aurea', others with a generous helping of gold like *I. aquifolium* 'Golden van Tol' or *I.a.* 'Golden Milkboy', whose leaves reverse the visual sequence with yellow at the centre and green at the edges. And I've no time for garden snobs who consider the golden hollies a bit naff. The hollies tolerate partial shade but you'll get better colour effects with full sun. They're not that fussy about soil conditions either, needing just reasonably fertile and well-drained conditions. For berries, you must make sure that you have male and female plants in your garden or at least in the vicinity. Holly is not just for Christmas, but for year-round delight.

POT-POURRI

P ot-pourri implies a mixture and that is what we have in this section of the book. And yet it has a thread running through it, which is my firm belief that gardening belongs to the whole and not part of life. My short spell as a gardening columnist came to an end because I couldn't adopt tunnel-like vision and write about grow-bags and when to prune your roses when subjects like gardens as table decorations or flowers in dress opened such extraordinarily more enriching vistas of perception and appreciation. But then we live in an age seemingly dedicated to dumbing down to the lowest common denominator of ignorance instead of lifting the reader up to something higher by opening windows in his or her mind.

What fascinates me about plants and gardens is that you can never quite escape them. They are invasive. When, for instance, you sit down to eat, ten to one it is from flower-sprigged china. And more often than not there's a floral centrepiece, formalised flowers and leaves on the wallpaper or on the room's textiles, perhaps too on the ceiling in the plasterwork and on the floor in the carpet. I pass over vases of flowers and pot plants. Move into the kitchen and the produce of the garden and orchard stare you in the face. Go upstairs into the bathroom and you will be adding flower fragrance to the bath water or savouring it in the perfumed soap. I will refrain from continuing the tour any further.

Nor can you escape gardens on stage or in literature or art. There is the lover pursuing the object of his desires in the *Roman de la Rose* and there, centuries later, is poor Elizabeth Bennett being told by Lady Catherine de Burgh that she has a very small park. Where would art be without the Dutch flower piece or Monet's apotheosis of Giverny? Such resonances catch the imaginaion and fascinate. What is depressing about so much gardening writing and so many gardening programmes today is that the garden is lowered and demeaned, diminished in stature. I cringe when I hear hints on how to make a wellington boot into a plant container. Is this what gardening has come to?

GARDENING CLOTHES

'Come dressed like peasants.' That is always my injunction to anyone coming to see the garden, for peasants they will seemingly meet as my wife and I stand in our gardening clothes to welcome them. Gardening clothes are special. They're the kind of garments that enter that league of aristocratic status encountered in young men of ancient family who are still wearing their grandfather's tail coat or shooting tweeds. In the case of clothes for the garden, I recall the extraordinary pile proffered the visitor by that great plantswoman Valerie Finnis, Lady Scott. The most distinguished garment in that accumulation stands up in its own mud and is bestowed only on people she esteems worthy of such a horticultural mantle. As her husband died in his ninety-ninth year it would be interesting to know the exact date of that particular piece of historic clothing.

On the whole, what one wears are cast-offs. My wife's winter gardening coat was the one she wore to be interviewed in for the Royal College of Art at the beginning of the 1950s. She now girds it at the waist with string. Her woolly hat was sent by an American friend who lives near Boston and who spends some of her time knitting them as a charity to hand out to road sweepers during the winter months. When it's warmer, Julia reverts to her smock period. Those garments are so seventies, reflecting exactly that decade's cult of the Arcadian rural life, but they're still great to garden in, with pockets along the front to carry what you need.

My pile looks like a male fashion throwaway from the sixties and seventies. For years I wore a wonderful pale cream corduroy jacket with pockets with huge flaps and a broad belt. In 1968 it was the acme of Carnaby Street trendiness. When that fell to pieces I donned a donkey-coloured Aquascutum overcoat, a relic from the same era. It was abbreviated to just below the knee and had a Regency cut of collar. I vividly recall when it was new, wearing it to go to lunch with Cecil Beaton and his murmurs of appreciation. Now the lining hangs in ribbons, a button or two is missing, and it's absolutely filthy. On warmer days I put on a brown close-cut anorak covered in white zips at the front, sleeves and pockets and lined with some heat-retaining fibreglass so that it crackles as I move. Turning over our scrapbooks for 1972 I can see myself standing there wearing it on our Tuscan honeymoon in the depths of Chiantishire in January, with a mile-long bright red scarf looped over it. As a piece of clothing that at least has a timeless quality. So much of the rest has only curiosity value.

High on that list would come the wearing-out of flared jeans in the garden. Some of mine were so wide at the bottom that they engulfed the shoe. Mercifully I'd worn them through by the early eighties, when even a glimpse of such a piece of clothing would have been an aberration. For a long time I've had a drawer for garden clothes and for years it's been the same corduroy jeans for winter and cast-off blue jeans for summer. But none of these carry the sentiment of the outer garments. I wear woolly hats too in winter; my mother was forever knitting them from oddments and now she has gone, they form more than a memory.

What you can't have enough of is boots and shoes and whatever form they take, fashion cast-offs are the last thing you need. I have to add that one of my favourite garden-writers, Katherine S. White, author of *Onwards and Upwards in the Garden* (a gathering of articles which she wrote for the *New Yorker* in the 1960s) would wander out in her best Ferragamo shoes! In summer I stick to wearing out any discarded trainers or slip-ons, while in winter it's cloggies and wellingtons. None of the latter ever last. Sooner or later you peer down and they've split. Worse, they spring a leak while you're wading through mud. That is why you can't have enough of them. In the back hall there are racks of footwear for the garden and that's for a very simple reason. Any gardener has to cope not only for himself but also for every visitor. We keep a fair range of foot sizes to hand, ready for all comers. The same applies to the mound of coats and waterproof covering.

What about gloves? Having struggled for years with my hands made elephantine and awkward by being encased in leather, I now opt for buying bundles of bright yellow stretch-vinyl ones when I can find them. But, I have to confess, most of the time I don't wear gloves at all because I love the feel of everything from petal, to leaf, to the earth itself. The result is gardener's hands I'm afraid – but who cares?

I'd add to that a stack of umbrellas. Every time I buy

aftershave I seem to get another free umbrella and I've no objection to being an advert for Aramis traversing the garden. But the galaxy includes everything from spoke-shattered city-gent-type umbrellas to a vast wooden oiled-canvas peasant's brolly from Italy. There's not time for fashion in the garden, which is such a relief.

ANTIQUE TOOLS

Antiques in the garden toolshed? Well, you have been warned. Few gardeners are aware that they may be using a highly desirable collectable, or that their grandfather's decrepit spade is worth a pound or two. Twenty-five years ago, I was lured by an antiques dealer in Burford, Gloucestershire, to see an Elizabethan flowerpot, but that was about it. It wasn't something that I'd given much thought to until the sale of the contents of West Green House, Hampshire, things which had been collected by Alastair MacAlpine, a perceptive and original snapper-up of trifles. The catalogue contained a fair sprinkling of Victorian zinc watering cans and glass cloches, going on to garden rollers, wheelbarrows and plant labels. It came as a bit of a surprise. That must be a decade ago by now and things have moved on a lot since.

I was made aware of just how much they'd moved on during a trip to see gardens in Normandy. One of those visited belonged to an ebullient young man called Guillaume Pellerin. It was not long before he revealed that the attic of

Château de Vauville was stuffed to the eaves with historic garden implements. Everything was there from spades to dibbers, from wheelbarrows to pruning knives. And in abundance, the result of a long obsession with the subject and of years of poking around both the Paris flea market and others nearer to home. But before you dismiss this as an eccentric aberration I should add that he applies the term 'antique' to all tools up to 1950, when plastic took over and mechanisation was on the way. He has produced, moreover, an elegant, profusely illustrated book in which his trophies are displayed, entitled *Garden Tools* (1996).

It's rare, of course, to find anything much before the nineteenth century, although the odd stone roller might still be lying around unspotted. But for the most part it's the rich harvest of implements produced for the nineteenth-century bourgeois gardening boom to which manufacturers fully responded. I'd no idea that there were so many exotic implements. There's a roguing fork to remove rogue plants from a crop, a dock and daisy grubber, a parsnip fork, a flower gatherer for a conservatory and the range of secateurs is mind-blowing. Old hedge trimmers look like a line-up of instruments used by a medieval torturer. The grace of old rakes I find deeply seductive, with their thin handles flexible to gather up hay or grass. Their appeal cannot be denied. One sighs, looking at the glint of metal where it has been worn through work, and at the indentation on the handles made through constant use. Such erosions are monuments to human toil in the garden which, in a way, sanctifies them.

By now I'm sure that many readers are about to leap out of their chairs and make their way to the garden shed, for who knows what lurks there, especially if the house is an old one. Tools tend to linger on even when discarded. The most one would do with a defunct spade would be to transform the handle into a dibber by sharpening it to a point. My own mind turns to a metal rolling water tank of a kind which can accommodate twelve gallons and which came in during the Victorian period. Ours came from my wife's aunt and dates, I believe, from the 1920s. From time to time we still use it and now I think, should I? Will I be eroding its value, like taking sandpaper to the Chippendale? Then there's the garden roller, cast-iron and massive, and never used – who ever would these days? That descended via my parents-in-law's house, which takes the roller back before 1914. And finally there's that cache of beautiful old country house clay pots I was given. Dare I use them?

Heaven knows I don't want the garden to become a museum, but I've suddenly been made aware that these tools have graduated to being art objects and that perhaps my casual attitude to them ought to change. But what does one do with them? Iron rusts and wood decays if it is left in the open or kept in the damp. Old watering cans and clay pots look magical just left around as garden still life, so deeply satisfying that one's memories are stirred. But the fragile items could be mounted in a pattern on the wall of a garden room or conservatory or, if one was lucky enough to have a capacious sitting area or sun lounge, arranged as curiosities. The moral is the usual one: don't throw anything away. Today's trug from the garden centre is tomorrow's museum piece, but I'm less sure about the petrol-driven shears and the shredder!

EMBROIDERED GARDENS

When evenings have drawn in, and gardening hours have contracted, my horticultural life begins to tread other paths. One of them is stitchery. About fifteen years ago I passed out in public through overwork and during convalescence took up tapestry. One floral carpet and too many cat-and blossom-laden cushions later, I find myself stitching two auriculas, one square panel out of the eight or more other flowers I need to complete before the next carpet arrives.

The relationship of embroidery to gardening has always fascinated me. I recall years ago my surprise when researching for a book on English Renaissance gardens, on discovering a Jacobean writing master who kept a shop in Blackfriars, and whose pattern books included designs not only for embroidery but 'For Joyners and Gardeners . . . Knots, and Buildings, and Morysies, and Termes'. Anyone who has looked at designs for knot gardens, let alone planted one, which I have, will know how conscious one becomes of the interplay between decorative motifs in any historical period. On visiting an Elizabethan house, one sees those knots turn up again in the plasterwork and marquetry as well as on dresses in portraits. It is an interesting window into the past as to how people got their garden designs, explaining too that wonderful unity of vision which drew together house and garden and which is all too often missing in our own era of design options.

That link of the two arts was to be even stronger in the baroque century which followed. The supreme garden set piece was the *parterre de broderie*, the embroidered parterre, a design in cut turf, clipped box, gravel and coloured stuffs which depicted a scrolling pattern of formalised arabesques, leaf shapes and flowers. Only with the advent of the landscape style did this overt connection between the two arts become less perceptible.

I have been struck by how often people who take to the needle are in fact very good gardeners. I think of the composer William Walton's widow Susannah, plying her needle across a vast copy of one of the Stoke Edith hangings. These record the formal garden at its height, with fountains, statues, parterres and exotic plants in Chinese blue and white pots. (Stoke Edith, Herefordshire, burned down in the 1920s.) The originals belong to the V & A, but are at Montacute House, Somerset, a National Trust property, and more than worth a visit. That is her winter work. Outside stretches that masterpiece she and her husband created with the help of Russell Page, La Mortola on Ischia. Then there's Sir Hardy Amies, stitching on to cushions designs for knots which were in the gardens of his heroine, the Winter Queen. Outside there is his own essay in perfect small garden-making. And there's the remarkable Kaffe Fassett, a devoted gardener, who gathers his blossoms and casts them across his extraordinary tapestry designs.

So not for nothing did William Morris, the great Victorian designer, liken embroidery to 'gardening with silk and gold thread'. His gardens were revolutionary in their time, rejecting the gaudy bedding-out of the high Victorian era and choosing to evoke, both at the Red House, Kent, and at Kelmscott Manor, Oxfordshire, gardens of the type he had glimpsed in medieval manuscripts and faded ancient tapestries. His embroidery designs for hangings and cushions were ambassadors for his garden style, popularising interest in wild flowers and old-fashioned native plants. His greatest disciple was Gertrude Jekyll, whose influence is still with us. We often lose sight of the fact that she began her career designing and executing embroideries, abandoning that for garden design only when her eyesight failed her.

Earlier in the century the wife of John Loudon, that prolific garden writer for the new middle classes, pointed out that progression in her book *The Villa Garden*, published in 1850 and a monument to the style Gertrude Jekyll detested. Jane Loudon wrote: 'There is not any lady who can design a pattern and embroider a gown, that might not, in few hours, be taught to design flower gardens with as much taste and skill as a professional landscape gardener.' *Voilà* Miss Jekyll.

Both skills call for a strong sense of good design and for a subtle control of colour. Both demand neatness, discipline and order. Winter is a good time if not to take to the needle at least to visit museums and galleries with embroidery collections. The whole history of garden design and plants is writ large in tapestries and stumpwork pictures, samplers and bed hangings, upholstery and Berlin woolwork. That such things are an inspiration to the gardener one can gather from the large Flemish tapestry of a Renaissance garden which still hangs immediately above Vita Sackville-West's writing desk at Sissinghurst. How often she must have looked up at it for a fresh green thought over the decades.

— ❖ —

BULB CATALOGUES

Bulbs in August – whatever next? With all those golden flowers, the ligularias, rudbeckias, helianthemums, and heleniums, reaching their apogee, it's standing the seasons on end to turn one's mind to next year's tulips, daffodils, hyacinths and narcissi. But you must. The assault on one's eyes, let alone one's cheque book, begins at the Chelsea Flower Show in May, where all the great bulb nurseries play on one's basest acquisitive instincts. Somehow they manage to hold their bulbs back from flowering so that we are able to experience the height of springtime again cheek by jowl with the roses of summer. Such displays are when you need your notebook to hand. So, too, is spring garden visiting invaluable, not to mention the Dutch bulb fields. Few other garden flowers remind one so much that gardening is hard commerce and the visual rape of Chelsea is followed swiftly after by the thud on to the doormat of the bulb catalogues in June. They again are designed to appeal to every latent predatory instinct.

Bulbs in a garden are an expensive business, so I'm rather relieved that it's my wife who plans and looks after this particular annual order. To make one at all you must have a plan, not just a vague one in your head but a loose-leaf file in which you have actually drawn a ground plan of your bulb planting. Add to that, in this day and age of cheap photography, photographs of each area in flower, even those planted naturalistically. Indeed it is those areas which it is always the most maddening to plan for. All through the flowering season Julia is busy snapping away to remind her just where the gaps are, particularly in the section we call the

Glade at the front of the house, that flower-dappled space which we look down upon from our bedroom window. The long grass is not cut until mid-August, by which time decisions will have been reached on gaps which have occurred in terms not only of space but also of flowering period. The panorama of flower – crocuses, chionodoxas, fritillaries, dwarf daffodils and iris, ending with martagon lilies – that manages to roll on from the first week in January to June is a joy, because we see it first thing in the morning as we get up. Always remember to place a few bulbs where they can be seen even on the coldest winter day.

However small your garden, you should select bulbs which will flower in sequence through late winter well into spring. Make a list on a piece of paper, noting the flowering times. Over colour, I can't stress enough the importance of making notes at the spring shows and garden visiting. Don't believe what the catalogues say. Last year we ordered some 'Willem van Oranje' tulips which turned out red! Seeing is believing. Also, if you're starting out with a small budget, you will be horrified at the cost of bulbs. Around £10 to £15 for thirty tulips seems about the norm, and believe me thirty won't go far. Even in the smallest town garden you won't make any impact with an initial expenditure under £200. Which brings me back to planning, because you need to think long term, adding each year in the case of a naturalistic planting. We have built up a breathtaking spring display in our large orchard, but it has taken twenty years to achieve.

In the case of a formal planting of tulips, we reckon that they can be left *in situ* for up to five years, provided that they are fed with bonemeal, the seedheads snapped off after they have flowered, and their leaves and stems left to die down until they can be gently pulled away in midsummer. If your garden has more than one room, always choose different colours and different flowering times. For formal planting, measure the bed and work out on graph paper how many you will need at the correct spacing. There are wonderful opportunities here. Remember the tulips don't have to be all the same colour or type. You can fill a bed with two types and colours alternating or you can peg out a simple pattern like a star within a circle or a circle or oval within a rectangle. Tulips are always enhanced if set within a framework of glossy green box or placed against a rich dark evergreen.

The centre bed in our Rose Garden, which is planted with 'Angélique' and 'Mount Tacoma' tulips, is about ten feet in diameter and calls for three hundred bulbs to fill it to any effect. So you can see the expense involved and also why we only replant every five years. In the case of tulips, don't scatter plant them. If your pocket is a bit eroded at the moment, far better to buy thirty and place them in a container where they will catch the eye from the house. This essay sounds money-obsessed but it needs to be. It is well worth shopping around for bulbs because the prices vary wildly from one firm to another, so much so that it is difficult to understand how the same item can vary differ in price so much. I would always recommend buying them by mail order rather than going to a garden centre. The specialist suppliers will have stored them at the right temperature, one far removed from the sales hot house.

Even when they're delivered in November in time to plant, your problems won't end there. There are nibbling mice to come and you can be sure that in the middle of your glorious bed of yellow tulips there'll be one which is bright red! All I can say is that we have never regretted money spent in this way. It is an investment in pure joy.

TABLE GARDENS

It was Francis Bacon, philosopher and Lord Chancellor, who in his famous essay 'Of Gardens' wrote: 'As for the Making of Knots, or Figures, with Divers Coloured Earths . . . You may see as good Sights, many times, in Tarts.' This dismissive comment in fact contains a grain of truth, for the earliest pictures I know of English tart decorations, in Robert May's *The Accomplisht Cook* (1661), shows a whole selection of designs for tarts and cheesecakes which virtually duplicate those for flowerbeds in books on garden design of the same period.

That kind of fascinating relationship between the table and the garden has been explored in a number of exhibitions in recent years. Those, however, which actually reconstruct accurately one of these fantastic table gardens are rare. One such was an exhibition at Fairfax House in York entitled 'The Pleasures of the Table', which was mounted at a time of the year when gardening largely consists of putting things to bed for the winter. Perhaps that explains the attraction in times past of transforming for a festive occasion a dining-room table into a formal garden in full bloom. Somehow it must have brought summer into winter.

The grandest set piece in the exhibition was a table laid for dessert, based on one of the designs from the middle of the eighteenth century, published by the great French cook, Menon, in 1749. Down the middle of the table a sheet of mirror glass had been laid and on it sat a classical temple of sugar, flanked by an elaborate swirling baroque parterre made of coloured sugar sands contained in pasteboard shapes, covered with silk chenille and interspersed with sugar statuary. Dessert was the finale to a very grand dinner, consisting of candied fruits, ice creams and other sweetmeats arranged *en tableau*. Now what was also striking was the fact that the plates themselves were botanical ones, or at least decorated with flowers. The first time I saw such a recreation it was a revelation not only about eating in times past, but about garden style and how flowers on ceramics were not merely decoration but part of an overall scene. Those who sat at this feast probably talked gardens and discussed the plants on the plates, many of which would have been new arrivals from the Americas.

This decorative dialogue with the table goes back a long way. At the Burgundian court in the fifteenth century there were such displays. 'Thirty plateaux in the manner of gardens' adorned the ducal table on the occasion of Charles the Bold's marriage to Edward IV's sister in 1468, along with trees 'of all sorts, of which the fruit and flowers are so cleverly made that they seem to be real trees and real fruits and very beautiful . . .' As the confectioner's art reached its apogee everything for a table garden could be purchased at a shop. The Duke of Gordon purchased a complete kit in 1765, including flowers, trees, eighteen pieces of parterre, all in sugar, and porcelain figures for the statuary. Note the latter, for all those eighteenth-century figurines of gardeners, shepherds and shepherdesses, the seasons and classical gods and goddesses, began their life often as part of one of those sugar and marzipan gardens. The fashion was still going strong in the 1780s. Dear greedy Parson Woodforde, the diarist, records one at a dinner given by the Bishop of Norwich in 1783: 'A most beautiful Artificial Garden in the Center of the Table remained at Dinner and afterwards, it was one of the prettiest things I ever saw . . .'

The survival of whole table gardens is very rare, but there are two of glass in the Museo Correr in Venice which include fountains. When Christmas is in the offing, it's worth remembering as an idea. I once dressed a Christmas table at Thomas Goode's, to raise money for charity , doing it as one of these gardens linking a symmetrically arranged group of white porcelain *putti* with a hedge of artificial evergreen.

The other thing I noted at York was something called a parterre of fruit. This was straight out of the court of Louis XIV and recreated from a design of 1688 by Jean Berain, the leading decorator of the day. The fruit was placed in different-shaped straw baskets which were composed in such a way that when arranged on the table they made up what was known as an English parterre. At the centre there was a chaplet of flowers, from the midst of which arose a pot with a stately orange tree. The table was garlanded with swags of flowers but was worth seeing for the authentic fruit, which was displayed in the baskets, as much as for this evocation of a lost garden form.

POLITICS IN THE GARDEN

Is there such a thing today as politics in the garden? At first glance, all I can think of is the rope-ringed rusticated column designed by Quinlan Terry for Lord McAlpine when he lived at West Green House. The Latin inscription on this fifty-foot high folly reads in translation: 'This monument was built with a great deal of money which otherwise would have been given into the hands of the Inland Revenue.' Erected in 1976 it marked the abandonment by the then socialist government of its proposed wealth tax. Mercifully his lordship had moved on before he could fulfil his 1979 intent of erecting a classical triumphal arch in honour of the 'first lady Prime Minister of Great Britain'.

In these garden fantasies McAlpine was only reviving an old British tradition, one in which an aristocrat's garden could resemble a horticultural election manifesto. Its heyday was the early eighteenth century and its greatest surviving example is (as I write) being handsomely restored by the National Trust. Lord Cobham's Stowe, in Buckinghamshire, is a political landscape, an attack on the prevailing Whig hegemony and a celebration of 'the liberty of Britain'. The Temple of British Worthies, with its busts of Milton, Shakespeare, Bacon, Locke and King Alfred among others, exulted those who had opposed 'slavish systems' of any kind. Later in that century we have what current garden historians categorise as Tory landscape, one which fanned out from the mansion house rearranging park, village, church and everything else in view to breathe an aura of timeless continuity, romantic sensibility and unbroken tradition.

The landscape style, which was born at the opening of that

era, was cast then as indeed it still is now as a national style reflecting native ideas of constitutional liberty as expressed in the Glorious Revolution of 1688. The formal gardens which preceded them with their regimented topiary, stately avenues, and elaborately patterned parterres laid out on a strictly symmetrical grid system were re-cast as evidence of the type of despotism that existed on the Continental mainland.

Which brings my thoughts winging to our own age. Was there any connection between the Conservative hegemony of the 1980s and early 1990s and the revival of formality in garden design? It is, I believe, an intriguing question, although I cannot pretend to produce a definitive answer. After all, the first public acceptance of the modern asymmetrical style stemming from the post-war influence of landscape architects, Roberto Burle Marx and Thomas Church was in that *ville imaginaire* of socialist ideals, the Festival of Britain in 1951. This was the style that landscape architects were to deploy in the new towns, estates and leisure centres of the new democratic Britain. Formality was seen to smack of the old aristocratic order of things.

It is, therefore, easy to see how that apostle of the new Utopia in landscape design Dame Sylvia Crowe, in her hugely influential book *Garden Design*, (1958) could reconcile these impulses with the sinuous waterlines and free curves of the eighteenth-century style. In this way, a style which was dedicated to the display of property rights and private interest was stood on its head and, shrunk down to the size of a postage stamp, was to become the formula for the average suburban rectangle. In a strange way, 'Capability' Brown, the modernist movement and the welfare state dream became interconnected.

If the landscape style accumulated overtones of the Left, can we argue that country house formality donned the weeds of the Right? Strangely enough formality, which had always been covertly kept going (even Sylvia Crowe had a yen for Hidcote), crept up the agenda during the ideological renaissance of the Right in the 1970s. Simultaneously, those high priestesses of Tory gardening formality Gertrude Jekyll and Vita Sackville-West were rediscovered and embraced by a huge gardening public. Both held views of society which were feudal, Jekyll writing about Surrey peasants and Sackville-West despising any who were not, to use her code word, 'bedint'. The old pre-1914 formal country house style began its long ascendancy, marking yet another example of middle England being conquered by aristocratic style. In this it was aided by the heritage cult and by what I would guess to be the new high Tory priestesses of formality, the Marchioness of Salisbury, Rosemary Verey and the late Alvilde Lees-Milne. In short, did Thatcher's Britain, as one long celebration of the extension and reassertion of private property rights, find its perfect garden expression in the explosion of clipped box parterres and knots, geometric potagers, avenues of pleached trees and laburnum tunnels evoking the country house Arcady of a pre-socialist Britain? If so, maybe Lord McAlpine should have built that arch after all.

INHERITED GARDENS

What happens when a private garden masterpiece changes hands? I wouldn't claim that perhaps for The Laskett yet, but as we both get older we do ponder on providing for its eventual fate. The problem was brought home to us by two recent garden experiences, one at Shute House and the other at Cranborne Manor, within striking distance of each other on the borders of Wiltshire and Dorset. In each case, the shift in ownership has taken a different form, Shute being a private house changing hands on the open property market, Cranborne being caught up in the inexorable migration of an aristocratic dynasty as the next generation moves into the great house. In both instances the incomers have taken on gardens which will always figure in any future history of garden-making in this country since 1945.

Cranborne Manor is a country house built by Robert Cecil, Earl of Salisbury, at the opening of the seventeenth century. Small in scale and built of mellowed stone and brick, it is the quintessence of 'The Mansions of England in the Olden Time'. It is a timeless English vision, the house nestling in a hollow held in by an amphitheatre of immemorial trees. Stretching out from the Jacobean house is a series of rooms etched in by handsome dark green yew hedges, each with its individual planting scheme. The original garden goes back to the period of the house when one of the earliest of plant hunters, John Tradescant, is known to have done some work there. The so-called Mount Garden, with a sundial on an eminence in its midst, is given to him, but the earliest certainly datable garden space is the fabulous walled North Garden which must be late seventeenth century; a formal enclosure with a terrace, and a grass walk leading to handsome gate piers flanked by ancient espaliered apples underplanted with pinks, the rest framed by borders filled with no other colours but green and white. The North Garden is of an unforgettable beauty even when looked at through a cloudburst.

That is how I remember it when I made my first inspiring visit in 1976. Then I wrote in my diary: 'The most perfect small-scale country-house garden I have ever seen, delicate, sensitive, English . . . ' That heyday was owed to the energetic garden style of the present Lady Salisbury, whose forceful statement of historical revivalism was aligned to a deep commitment to the organic cause. But in 1992 she moved on to Hatfield and her daughter-in-law Lady Cranborne, also a passionate gardener, took on the inheritance. There used to be a tiny knot garden filled with all the flowers known to John Tradescant but it has gone. On my recent visit, I felt a pang of sadness about that. The forecourt, too, has been altered to a circle of York stone and old brick planted with alpines; windows have been cut into hedges; a stone bridge over a little stream has vanished; and much of the planting has changed. I stood transfixed, mourning what was no more, things which had inspired me; and then I thought, no, a garden is all about change. The incoming generation must make their contribution, and that, too, when the time comes, will undergo the same fate.

Now Shute presents a different scenario. This was commissioned by Michael and Lady Anne Tree from Sir Geoffrey Jellicoe in 1969 and indeed he regarded it as his favourite private garden. As usual with Jellicoe, one is deep into Jung and primal mythic forces, in this instance a miraculous essay on a tiny scale, three acres, on water. The *tour de force*, which is famous, is the small cascade that, as it descends, changes into a rill of the kind found in the Mogul gardens in Kashmir. Next in importance comes the rectangular canal which was presided over by three terms depicting the Augustan poets, Virgil, Ovid and Lucretius. These were the philosophical basis of the meaning of the garden, asking the visitor to remember the classical pastoral tradition. Their poems record metamorphoses of people into water, trees and plants. The new owners, Mr and Mrs John Lewis, did not acquire the poets which have been replaced by three splendid baroque busts of Apollo, Diana and Neptune. So the keys to the meaning of the garden have already gone, but can you blame the new owners? They are not after all museum curators. A garden can survive unaltered only if it is adequately endowed and given over to a body like the National Trust. Even then it can never quite be static. But if a private garden changes hands it has to be made to work for the new owners and change must come. Shute is fortunate in that Mr and Mrs Lewis are enthusiastic admirers of Jellicoe's work and have set about the costly task of making many of the leaking ponds watertight. The cascade and rill they have already restored to its pristine state and indeed it looks as stunning as the many pictures of it. But the Lewises have to live there and are making their own contribution. I can't blame them for sweeping away Lady Anne's whimsical topiary four-poster, or for beginning to rethink the six large box-edged flowerbeds which I thought curiously dull and sadly lacking in articulation or verticals. And anyway, I always remember Jellicoe saying that the last thing he was interested in was flowers!

For most gardeners such a problem does not arise. We come and we go. But for a handful, the decisions must be painful and far from easy, for these new owners have in their hands Britain's late twentieth-century garden heritage. It is a less enviable mantle than it would at first glance seem.

FOREVER ENGLAND

The bus stopped and disgorged about thirty members of the Garden History Society's tour of Portugal outside a pair of gothic gate piers giving on to a path which curved its way sharply downwards. We were about to enter an English garden abroad, one of the two – the other is La Mortola – greatest. Montserrate, near Sintra, was a dual creation, first of the fantastic William Beckford, of Fonthill Abbey fame, and later of the more prosaic Sir Francis Cook, the textile millionaire. Between them, they were to transform an eighty-acre valley into paradise, initially in the newfangled picturesque style, and then as a monument to plant hunters.

In many ways, these two men epitomised the English gardener abroad: arrogant, super-rich, plant mad, often to the point of lunacy, and with a disdain for the horticultural traditions of the native, to whom was consigned the role of providing the cheap labour essential to such stupendous enterprises.

Montserrate today has all the makings of a tragedy: the project to restore and preserve it for posterity has foundered in the treacherous sea that is Portuguese bureaucracy. It needed some prompting to discover this from the young English designer, Gerald Luckhurst, who had headed the scheme and was our guide on this rainswept April day. Between showers, we made our way up and down precipitous paths and winding walkways, aware that we were probably looking our last on a peerless garden.

The original house had been built by an English merchant of Huguenot extraction, Gérard de Visme, in the gothic style, the earliest of its kind in the country. In the 1850s, Cook was to overlay this chaste edifice with decoration, much as one would ice a cake.

The landscape is the work of Beckford, who lived here on and off for fifteen years, during the Napoleonic wars. He constructed the dramatic cascade, framed by two large pines, which tumbles in a torrent into the valley below. On a nearby ledge, he re-erected as a ruin the remains of a gothic church destroyed in the Lisbon earthquake of 1755. His was a garden of the kind popularised by Sir Uvedale Price and Richard Payne Knight, exponents of the picturesque.

But this was only a preliminary foray compared with the long reign of Cook and his descendants from 1856 to 1929, the year of the financial crash. With him came the plantsman's utopia, for he collected trees and shrubs as others collect postage stamps. With an army of more than seventy gardeners, Cook made Montserrate Portugal's Kew. The skeleton of the gargantuan irrigation system carrying water to every plant is still there, as are most of his treasures, the exotic conifers, evergreen trees, shrubs and ferns, which so appealed to the Victorians.

Montserrate sums up the glory and the vulnerability of English gardens abroad, quintessential manifestations of an era when England's garden style and horticultural expertise marched hand-in-hand with its commercial dominance and imperial expansion. And we are fortunate that in the nick of time, they have found their master chronicler, Charles Quest-Ritson, whose superbly researched and stylishly written account, *The English Garden Abroad* (1992), will be the classic treatment of its subject.

As he writes, Montserrate is not alone in its fate. La Mortola, on the Riviera dei Fiori, the work of successive generations of Hanburys, now belongs to the University of Genoa. It is faring well compared with Montserrate, but the Italians find it difficult to respond to the uniquely English aesthetic such a composition epitomises.

Lawrence Johnston's La Serre de la Madone, above Menton in France, lingers on as a plundered, despoiled remnant, all but inaccessible. The Villa Malfitano in Palermo, laid out in the 1890s by the Whitakers, a family of merchants, is an extraordinary late-Victorian essay in the gardenesque, but is in a critical state, with overgrown paths, choked water courses, the grotto engulfed with weeds and the seedlings of invasive trees spelling worse disasters to come.

In their heyday, during the century after 1850, these gardens were extraordinary, the expressions of wealth and a way of life made possible by the growth of modern communications. The Cooks, for example, only ever saw their garden for two months a year. These gardens abroad were mainly seasonal, designed to be in tip-top condition for the arrival of the owners escaping the rigours of the English winter. In the case of the French Riviera, the season ended on 21 April, when residents returned home in time for a very different season, the London one.

These gardens also had an attraction beyond mere display, for it was possible to grow plants in the open that at home belonged only in the greenhouse and conservatory. Rare plants were not only evidence of botanical commitment and knowledge but a sign of wealth, as gathering them required worldwide connections.

The English gardens created in Tuscany have the best chances of survival. This is partly because it was the English who rediscovered for the Italians their own garden history. They leased and bought old villas and laid out gardens appropriate to their architectural period, with terraces, staircases, balustrading, fountains, statuary and topiary in abundance, but overlaid with a planting which could only be English.

No area has held the English captive more than Tuscany. This is the world of *A Room with a View*. It was also one which found its architect in Cecil Pinsent. For forty years, from Bernard Berenson's I Tatti to his masterpiece for the writer Iris Origo and her husband at La Foce, Pinsent gave villa owners his synthesis of Italianate historicism combined with the lush planting of an Edwardian country house in the Home Counties.

The casualties here are fewer. La Foce is still there to be marvelled at with its stately evergreens and, above all, its plants, shrubs and climbing roses, honeysuckle and jasmine trailing everywhere, and wild flowers in profusion. So, too, is I Tatti, albeit institutionalised.

If I had to choose a favourite, however, it would be Ninfa, below Sermoneta, just south of Rome. How long it will survive may be open to question, but a trust exists to secure its future. I have seen it in spring and in autumn. Both visits were magical experiences, but it is the idea behind Ninfa above everything else that exerts an unforgettable spell, lifting every visit to the level of the surreal. That idea was to turn a medieval town, abandoned in 1382, into a garden and, the ultimate coup, to enliven it with a stream from which rivulets flowed to every part. Any visit is like trespassing in Sleeping Beauty's palace, in which gates, arches, towers, walls, churches and houses are spangled with flowers – wisteria, honeysuckle, clematis, passion flowers and, above all, roses – which soar heavenwards only to cascade down again.

There are echoes of Sissinghurst, which also arose from a ruin, but there is no concession to the Italianate, not a clipped tree or a statue in sight. Ninfa seems to combine a landscape in the picturesque manner with planting of the kind popularised by William Robinson. In many ways, its closest equivalent is Scotney, in Kent, where the new mansion looks down on a garden incorporating the ruined castle. But, alas, for Ninfa there are no National Trust gardeners to ensure its future. In Italy it remains a horticultural aberration.

It is difficult to visit any of these gardens without being seized by a sense of time past and of a homecoming. However neglected, municipalised, institutionalised or just plain vandalised, there still lingers in them something which is forever England. A corner is turned and one's breath is caught as a vault of trees beckons one along a woodland walk fringed with wild flowers that could be in Cornwall. Or classical deities stare down bewildered on to a balustrade engulfed by a 'Dorothy Perkins' rose in a way no Italian would ever permit. Or clumps of flowers, part of a forgotten herbaceous border, struggle to raise their heads beneath the walls, making a tableau from the Cotswolds.

Moments such as these linger in the memory as poignant reminders that we have, too, lost an empire of flowers. We should be grateful that this vanished empire found its chronicler before all is dust.

CONDITOR HORTI FELICITATIS AUCTOR

GARDENING & HOPE

The Chelsea Flower Show in 1998 was the most brilliant I'd seen for many years. The sun shone, bestowing a golden glow across what is an annual explosion of foliage and flower right in the heart of the metropolis, and the water in the rills, fountains, ponds and cascades in the show gardens sparkled in the sunlight. I love it all, from the unattainable splendour of the show gardens to the lowly line-ups of garden mowers, from the tableaux of bonsai to the stands chocka with terracotta pots. But I love it even more for something else, which is true Brit: the people who come to it.

I sat there munching my Brie baguette just looking at the tide of humanity passing me by. There's everyone here, all sorts and conditions of us islanders. Up from the shires, from the suburbs, from the darkest recesses of our inner cities, they throng in their thousands. In fact, some thirty thousand a day, I'm told. The women can be dolled up as if they were about to open a garden party, all floral silk dresses and large hats, or equally they can be in straight-cut denim skirts and blouses with sensible flat shoes. The men can be elegantly besuited, sporting buttonholes and straw fedoras, or in short-sleeved shirts and crumpled trousers, sandals and an old cotton hat that's spent most of its life screwed up in a pocket. But they all share one thing in common, they're intent and they're smiling. Even more than that they are together.

To me that gathering is this country united. There's no tension, no sense of distance or division or any feeling of them or us. Gardening has become one of this island's miracles, an activity that cuts across the whole of society bringing us together with one single shared activity of hands in the soil. It has become glue of a kind which sadly neither the monarchy nor the church can achieve any more.

This is the most extraordinary phenomenon and the secret of its success is that it works from diversity and pluralism. That's not to say that garden style doesn't change as the gurus of design annually tell us what's out and what's in, but when it comes down to it, style doesn't matter. There's room for everyone in gardening and for every style. Even if your garden happens to be only a potted plant on the kitchen sill or a window box, you're welcomed in to the Temple of Flora. The range is terrific, from the lordly owner of a great landscape garden covering thousands of acres to the chap with a small allotment by a railway siding. Your garden can be in the cottage style or in the country house style. It can be a collection of containers on the terrace of a council flat in a tower block, or a fancy box parterre at the back of a smart Chelsea town house. It can equally be a wild organic haven, buzzing with birds, butterflies and bees, or a defiant blaze of bedded-out begonias and French marigolds. They are all gardens.

I refuse to allow snobbery in gardening. My criterion is: 'Does this give you pleasure and delight? Does this recharge your batteries and lift your spirit?' If it does that's fine, as far as I'm concerned, even if I'd run a mile from the result. I really don't care if plaster gnomes switch some gardeners on, as long as they get a thrill out of that most mysterious and taken-for-granted of things, a garden.

That sense of garden for Everyman is peculiarly British. It was an invention of the Victorian age when the population trebled in a century as men and women flocked, seeking work in the new industrial towns and cities. Yes, there were horrendous slums and there was appalling social injustice and poverty but there also emerged terraces of little houses with tiny front and back gardens. That happened nowhere else in Europe as far as I know. Give thanks for it. Everyman was given a precious plot of earth on which to plant a flower and cultivate produce, a place to sit in the shade or in the sun resting from his labours, escaping from the grim side of urban life to look at the petals unfolding or the fruit ripening.

Both my grandparents had such houses. They had come to London in the 1880s. I still see in my mind's eye that patch of dark soil edged with scallop shells and the bouquet of white Japanese anemones silhouetted against the fence. Moving on I recall my father clipping the green privet hedge in front of the 1920s terrace house in which I was born. Every year a striped canvas curtain was put up to prevent the paint on the front door scorching, and from the porch hanging baskets would be suspended. Every evening there was the ritual watering. The border around the front lawn was planted with antirrhinums and edged with white and blue alyssum and lobelia. In the back garden Williams pear trees were espaliered against the fence and on the back of the garage grew a 'Paul's Scarlet Climber' rose arising above a rockery which surrounded a tiny rectangular pond filled with goldfish. My father would sit there each evening just dreaming. Elsewhere there were strings up which climbed scarlet runner beans, rows of onion and lettuce, and tomato plants from whose green fruit my mother made chutney. Up and down the country such gardens still go on, timeless in their way but embodying simple virtues not to be despised, ones which speak of self-sufficiency, domestic life and an appreciation of the realm of nature.

I'm aware that gardening is big business these days, with a multibillion-pound turnover in the garden centres. These offer you every horticultural delight and horror you can't afford. No, I don't despise them, for I often use them myself, but my heart's elsewhere, in gardening friendships expressed in the exchange of gifts of seeds, roots and cuttings, and in mutual garden visiting. A great gardener once said to me, 'Remember, it's very vulgar to buy plants.' And I can now see what she meant. I see it reflected in our version of what my mother-in-law called her garden of remembrance, that is the plants in the garden given to her by her friends. My wife and I often stroll through our own garden happily recalling this or that person by a tree, a shrub or some flowers. Some are people no longer with us, which makes the living plants all the more poignant.

Everyone recognises that there has been an explosion of interest in gardening. This applies not only to Britain but now also stretches across Europe into countries like Poland. Countries such as France and Italy, formerly very little interested, have become obsessed by it. But no one has quite explained why this extraordinary renaissance has occurred. To me it is a complex phenomenon, brought about by a mixture of motives, some more honourable than others. After doing up the home the garden would inevitably follow in what is a consumer society, so there is an element of keeping up with the gardening Joneses. But there's also a reawakening to our garden heritage, reflected in the ever-escalating numbers visiting our great historic gardens – so much so that many are in danger of being eroded. Television and radio must have contributed too. Then there's the ever-burgeoning garden literature, the cornucopia of mouth-watering books with inspirational pictures, not to mention the growing market for gardening magazines from down-to-earth *Gardener's World* to carriage-trade *Gardens Illustrated*.

Deep down I nurture a hope that it also reflects something profounder, the average person's attempt to cope with the problems of Planet Earth in an age which continues to see change on an unprecedented and bewildering scale, so much so that Everyman finds it beyond his comprehension. His response is often to cultivate his garden and I can understand why. There nature, unchanged since the Garden of Eden, pursues her annual cycle from life to death. Leaves and petals unfurl, flourish, fade and fall but they always spring to life again. In an unbelieving age, maybe this eternal cycle feeds the spirit in a way that the churches so often have failed to do. Nature is its own resurrection story.

People often ask me what is the most important thing that I've done with my life and I reply, 'To have made a garden.' And a garden jointly. I recall someone saying to me before I proposed to my wife that a marriage was made up of small things like planting a flower together. For me that has been true, although on a large scale! I suppose if you also asked what entrances me most about gardening after having been hooked on it for twenty-five years, the answer could be given in one word: hope. Every winter we live in hope that spring will come. This or that doesn't do as well one year as last but the hope is next year that it will do better. We plant in hope. We live in hope. What more can anyone ask of life?

INDEX

camellias, 93
Campbell, Susan, 131
Canons Ashby, 120
Caprarola, 86, 87
Carr, David, 29
Caserta, 85
Catalpa bignonioides, 35
catmint, 93
Cecil, Robert, 50, 198
chaenomeles, 93
Chambers, Sir William, 153
Charles the Bold, 193
Charles, Prince of Wales, 51, 152
Chelsea Flower Show, 29, 189, 209
Chelsea Physic Garden, 32-5, 38; cotton
  seeds from, 34; poisonous plants in,
  32; rockery in, 34-5; salvia in, 34
cherry trees, 105; morello, 104; wild,
  71
chionodoxa, 61
Church, Thomas, 196
Cicero, 15
Classic Garden Design, 29
Clarke, Ethne, 108
clematis, 93
Clematis montana 'Elizabeth', 149
Clement VII, Pope, 86
Clevely, A.M., 29
clothes, gardening, 180-3
Coade, Mrs, 87
Cobbett, William, 109, 172
colour, use of in gardens, 25, 46, 83,
  101-103
Cook, Sir Francis, 201
Cook family, 202, 203
Corpechet, Lucien, 38
Countrie Housewifes Garden, 109
Country Life, 133
Courances, 35-8
cow parsley, 61
Cranborne, Lady, 199

Cranborne Manor, 51, 120, 198
Crateagus monogyna, 89
Creating Small Formal Gardens, 29
Creating Topiary, 29
Crichel, 51
crocus, 101
Crowe, Dame Sylvia, 27, 81, 196, 197
Cupani, Father, 153
X *Cupressus leylandii*, 89, 93, 134
Cydonia oblonga 'Champion', 163; *C.o.*
  'Early Prolific', 163; *C.o.* 'Le
  Bourgeaut', 163; *C.o.* 'Lescovatz', 163;
  C.o. 'Ludovic', 163; 163; *C.o.* 'Meech's
  Prolific', 163, 164; *C.o.* 'Seibosa', 163;
  C.o. 'Vranja', 163
cypress, 43, 45
Czechoslovakia, 102

D

daffodils, 61; (*Narcissus*) 'White Lion', 61
dahlias, 40, 157-9;
Dahlia excelsa, 40
daisies, Michaelmas, 61, 158
Danvers, Sir John, 32
David, Elizabeth, 169
de Caus, Salomon, 86-7
de Villanueva, Juan, 38
de Visme, Gérard, 202
de Vries, Vredemann, 96
De Wiersse, 82
Den Nederlandtsen Hovenier, 96
Descartes, René, 37
Detached Sentences on Gardening, 69
Diana, Princess of Wales, 128
Dodoens, Rembert, 118
Dryden family, 120
Duchêne, Achille and Henri, 36
Duff, Lady Juliet, 82
Dürer, Albrecht, 70
Dutch gardens, Dutch gardeners, 22-5,
  30, 33, 59, 82, 96, 115, 139

E

Earle, Mrs, C.V. (Maria Theresa Villers), 131-3, 155-6
eleagnus, 9
Elizabeth I, 50, 61
Ellacombe, Canon Henry, 131
embroidery, of gardens, 186-8
English Flower Garden, The, 131, 148
English Garden Abroad, The, 203
English gardens abroad, 201-6
English Gardener, The, 109
English Husbandman, The, 59
Erysimum cheiri 'Blood Red', 143; *E.c.* 'Fire King', 143; *E.c.* 'Ivory White', 143; *E.c.* 'Persian Carpet', 143; *E.c.* 'Primose Bedder', 143
euonymus, 93
Evelyn, John, 32, 42, 172, 175

F

Fairchild, Thomas, 153
Fairfax House, 192
Fantin-Latour, Henri, 165
Farnese, Cardinal, 86
Fassett, Kaffe, 187
Fatsia japonica, 93
Festival of Britain, 196
Fiennes, Celia, 105
Financial Times, 30
Finnis, Valerie, Lady Scott, 180
Flora, 167
Flower and the Leaf, The, 171
Flower Garden, The, 153
Food in England, 157
Fontainbleau, 86; Fontaine du Tibre, 86
Fonthill Abbey, 201
Formal Garden in England, The, 29
Forsythe, William, 34
fountains, 36, 92; at Het Loo, 23; in Boboli Gardens, 42; at The Laskett, 55, 171; at Stoke Edith, 187; at Villa

Fontanelle, 65
Fowler, John, 28, 59
France, gardens in, French gardens, French gardeners, 35-8, 53, 86, 87, 97, 106, 118, 128, 165, 183-4, 203
Francini brothers, 86
Francis, Mark, 16
Frewin Hall, 62, 163
fritillaries, 61
Fruit Book, 173
fruit trees, 104-6
fuschias, 94

G

Galanthus, G. 'Atkinsii', 141; *G. graecus*, 141; *G. reginae-olgae*, 141; *G.* 'Mighty Atom', 141; *G.* 'Hill Poë', 141; *G. nivalis*, 142; *G. n.* 'Flore Pleno', 142
Gambara, Cardinal, 86
Ganay family, 35
Garden Craftsmanship in Yew and Box, 29
Garden Design, 29, 81, 196
garden history, 16, 28, 30, 32
Garden History Society, 28, 201
Garden Tools, 184
Gardener's Dictionary, 147
Gardens Old and New, 58
garlic, 168-70; *blanc*, 168, 169; *rose*, 168, 169; *violet*, 168, 169; pickled, 168; storing, 168
Garrya elliptica, 101
Garsington, 46
Gatacre, E.V., 82
Gatty, Mrs Alfred, 110
George VI, 115
Georgian gardens, 70, 103, 109
geraniums, as bedding, 67, 94; hardy, 63, 71
Gerard, John (Herbalist), 116-8, 147, 166
Gerard, John (Jesuit priest), 162
Germany, German gardens, 77-8, 87

ACKNOWLEDGEMENTS

The following articles, listed by publication in the order in which they appear in this book, first appeared in:

Chilstone Garden Ornaments Catalogue
Ornament

Country Life
Woodside

Daily Mail
Gardening and Hope

The Garden
Trompe l'Oeil

Gardens Illustrated
River Gods
Garden Arches

Good Housekeeping
Hatfield Old Palace

Hortus
The Laskett

House and Garden
Little Sparta

The Sunday Times
Topiary

The Times Saturday Review
The Palace of Het Loo
Forever England

And the following articles appeared in a regular column for the *Sunday Telegraph*:
The Chelsea Physic Garden; The Royal Botanic Gardens, Madrid; The Boboli Gardens, Florence; Pläs Brondanw; Green Theatres; Fruit Trees in the Flower Garden; Raised Beds; Timepiece; John Gerard; Mowing; Training Yew Hedges; Compost; Haircut Time; Wallflowers; Acanthus; Roses; Sweet Peas; Marigolds; Dahlias; Briar Roses; Quinces; Nasturtiums; Medlars; Holly; Embroidered Gardens; Bulb Catalogues; Table Gardens; Inherited Gardens

PUBLISHER'S ACKNOWLEDGEMENTS

EDITOR Julia McRae
ASSISTANT EDITOR Tom Windross
DESIGNER Sarah Pickering
INDEXER Stephen Hayward
HORTICULTURAL ADVISOR Tony Lord
ART DIRECTOR Caroline Hillier
EDITORIAL DIRECTOR Katherine Cave